INDIANAPOLIS THEN AND NOW

You can find most of the sites featured in the book on t

* The map and site location circles are intended to give readers a broad view of where the historic homes, landmarks, and other sites are located around downtown Indianapolis. Please consult a tourist map for greater detail.

Elyse & Chris,

    I cant express to the both of you how awesome its been to get to know the both of you over the years. From you being the first people to know about us being pregnant with Annie, to filming with HGTV, its truly been awesome. You both have been awesome clients and friends. While I'm super sad to see you leave Indy, I'm thrilled for this next chapter. I'm sure you'll love Seattle.

Enjoy this book as a way to keep the memories of Indy alive.

I'll miss you both and thanks for allowing me to be a part of your lives over the years.

                - Mike

INDIANAPOLIS

THEN AND NOW®

ACKNOWLEDGMENTS
Special thanks in the preparation of this book are extended to Tina Connor, Wanda
Willis, Jennifer Hanson, Bill Selm, James Glass, Bill Brooks, Michelle Laird, Jane Rulon,
Chris Pohl, Scott Truax, Cindy Highberg, and Robert Joseph. We would also like to
credit the following sources for providing information for this book: T*he Insider's
Guide to Greater Indianapolis* by Skip Berry and Jenny Phelps Ketzenberger, *The
Encyclopedia of Indianapolis* by Peter J. Bodenhamer and Robert G. Barrows, *The Main
Stem of North Meridian Street* by Peter J. Bodenhamer, Lamont Hulse, and Elizabeth
B. Monroe, *Indianapolis: Hoosiers' Circle City* by George A. Geib, *IUPUI: The Making of
an Urban University* by Ralph Gray, *Indianapolis Union Station* by James Hetherington,
Indianapolis Architecture by the Indianapolis Architecture Foundation, *Indianapolis:
The Story of a City* by Edward A. Leary, *Lost Indianapolis* by John P. McDonald, and *The
Circle: The Center of Indianapolis* by Ernestine Bradford Rose.

PICTURE CREDITS
The publisher wishes to thank the following for kindly supplying the photographs that
appear in this book:

"Then" Photographs:
Artemis Images/Indianapolis Motor Speedway: 92; Bettmann/CORBIS: 90;
BroadRippleHistory.com: 123 inset, 124; Crown Hill Cemetery Archives: 114; Evan Finch:
66 inset; Historic Landmarks Foundation of Indiana: 44, 47; Indiana Album: 62, 97, 137
(right); Indiana Fire Department: 15; Indiana Historical Society: 8, 12, 28, 34, 46, 56, 58,
60, 61 inset, 62, 68, 76, 88, 98, 102, 128, 132; Indiana Historical Society, Bass Collection
(negative numbers in brackets): 14 (310579-2), 16 (5172), 18, 20 (6514), 24 (26199), 26
(200470-F), 30 (24702), 32, 36 (238555-F), 40 (299683), 52 (17336), 54 (91531-F), 64 (4576),
72, 74 (A395), 78 (209352), 80, 82 (208021-F), 94 (69902-F), 96 (91622-F), 102 (228081-F),
104 (92875), 106 (5144), 108 (65877), 112, 116, 118 (201459-F), 122 (C30), 126 (321224-F),
136 (238280-F-E), 138 (26232), 140, 142 (93791); Indiana State Library: 10, 66, 84, 134;
IUPUI University Library Special Collections and Archives: 70, 86; Library of Congress:
11, 20 inset, 23, 38, 56 inset, 65, 74 inset, 76 inset, 91, 105, 110, 114 inset, 119, 137 left;
PK Partners: 130; Riley Museum Home: 42; Tim & Avi's Salvage Store: 50; University
Archives, Butler University Libraries: 120

"Now" Photographs:
All photographs were taken by Garry Chilluffo, ©Garry Chilluffo/Pavilion Image Library

About the photographer:
Garry Chilluffo, an Indianapolis-based commercial photographer, specializes in
architectural and advertising photography, with a personal interest in historic
preservation. Originally from upstate New York, he is a graduate of the Rhode
Island School of Photography and Winona School of Professional Photography. His
photography book projects include *The Art of the 92 County Walk* for the Indiana State
Museum, *Indianapolis Then and Now* (2004), and multiple updated editions for the
Then and Now series.

INDIANAPOLIS
THEN AND NOW®

NELSON PRICE AND JOAN HOSTETLER

"NOW" PHOTOGRAPHY
BY GARRY CHILLUFFO

English Hotel and Opera House, c. 1925   p. 14

Bates Block: The When, 1905   p. 20

Indiana and Capitol Theatres, 1929   p. 32

Marion County Courthouse, c. 1904   p. 38

Hammond Block, 1975   p. 47

Polk's Sanitary Milk Company, 1925   p. 54

Ruskaup Building, c. 1895   p. 60

Woodruff Place Fountain, 1905   p. 64

Wonderland Amusement Park, 1910   p. 66

The Barge, c. 1935   p. 68

Central Canal, c. 1953   p. 80

Walker Theatre, 1928   p. 82

Indianapolis Motor Speedway, c. 1915   p. 90

Federal Building, 1908   p. 94

Indiana War Memorial, 1932   p. 100

Tee Pee Restaurant, c. 1957   p. 116

Monon Railroad, c. 1950   p. 126

Indiana Statehouse, 1925   p. 142

INDIANAPOLIS

THEN AND NOW INTRODUCTION

When writers and visitors refer to the twelfth-largest city in America as "Indy," it's almost always with warmth and frequently followed by a remark about the sheer vitality of the place. The origins of the city can be traced to 1820, when Hoosier dignitaries gathered at early settler William Conner's log cabin on the White River near Noblesville to plan a new state capital. Corydon, which had been serving as the capital since Indiana achieved statehood in 1816, was judged to be too far south for statewide convenience. The new capital needed to be in the middle of the nineteenth state, the pioneer powerbrokers decided.

The undeveloped lowland that would become Indianapolis was chosen because of its central location. The next year, surveyor Alexander Ralston, who had helped design Washington, D.C., put forth a plan for Indiana's capital city that reflected the nation's. He laid out Indianapolis on a grid; a "Mile Square" was bounded by North Street, South Street, East Street, and West Street and four diagonal avenues radiated from a circle at the center of the Mile Square. The Governor's Mansion would be built in the center, surrounded by Circle Street.

This design didn't go to plan, however. The Governor's Mansion was built at the center, but no Indiana governor ever lived there. According to folklore, the reasons include early first ladies' objections to hanging their families' laundry, particularly undergarments, at the center of the city for all to see. Meanwhile, no sooner had residents arrived to build and settle in

Indianapolis than a malaria epidemic swept the city in 1821. The second physician to show up in town, Dr. Isaac Coe, blamed the epidemic on vapors from the swamps and lowlands on which the Hoosier capital was built.

From that inauspicious beginning, a bustling city did emerge. During the late 1800s and early 1900s, art and literature flourished, with national celebrities such as Pulitzer Prize–winning novelist Booth Tarkington and poet James Whitcomb Riley among the city's illustrious residents. Tarkington and other notables lived in magnificent mansions built during the 1920s on North Meridian Street; their restored homes remain showplaces nearly one hundred years later. The same goes for the enchanting Lockerbie neighborhood, which was Riley's home base when he wasn't crisscrossing the country on tour. Lockerbie, too, has been preserved. Visitors to today's Indianapolis invariably marvel at the neighborhood of cobblestone streets, white picket fences, and historic homes only a stroll away from downtown skyscrapers.

During the first half of the twentieth century, jazz music burst from clubs along legendary Indiana Avenue. During the day, teenagers like future novelist Kurt Vonnegut and future foreign policy expert Richard Lugar produced the nation's first daily high school newspaper, the Daily Echo, at a public school considered one of the finest in the land, Shortridge High School.

The inaugural Indianapolis 500 on May 30, 1911, placed a spotlight on the city as Americans got caught up in the car craze. Three decades of thrills ensued at the two-and-a-half mile, oval-shaped track. During World War II, though, the Indianapolis 500 was suspended. By 1946, the racetrack was nearly overgrown with weeds. Terre Haute businessman Tony Hulman came to the rescue when he bought the Speedway in 1946 and initiated a massive improvement campaign that propelled the Indianapolis 500 to glory years that surpassed those of the prewar era.

From the 1950s through the 1970s, though, downtown Indianapolis was lackluster, accounting for the city's nickname of "Naptown." The 1980s brought the beginning of an astonishing rejuvenation of the downtown area and an image overhaul. In 1984, the newly built RCA Dome (known then as the Hoosier Dome) became the home of the Indianapolis Colts, vaulting the city into major-league status, at least in the eyes of those who make assessments based on sports and cultural attractions. Next came a track record for hosting major events, including the exhilarating Pan American Games in 1987, which solidified Indy's reputation as the country's "amateur athletics capital" and helped established an international presence for the city. The Colts won the Super Bowl in 2007, one year before Lucas Oil Stadium opened as the team's new home, replacing the RCA Dome. In 2012, the city even served as the host of a wildly successful Super Bowl.

By then, Alexander Ralston's Mile Square had other gems, among them Circle Centre, a $307 million retail and entertainment complex that opened in 1995 amid much fanfare. Owned by the Indianapolis-based Simon Property Group, the nation's largest developer of shopping malls, Circle Centre incorporated facades of some historic downtown retail outlets even as other structures were demolished. Restaurants, nightclubs, and new or significantly enhanced museums opened downtown and in the nearby White River State Park area, providing alternatives to long-popular Broad Ripple dining spots, bars, and boutiques on the Northside. On sunny days, the Monon Trail, created from a reclaimed railroad right-of-way, bursts with runners, cyclists, in-line skaters, and walkers, as do the European settings along the scenic downtown canal of the White River, which now make Indy a vibrant place.

c. 1893

SOLDIERS' AND SAILORS' MONUMENT
Indiana's Civil War veterans
memorialized in the heart of the city

LEFT: The Soldiers' and Sailors' Monument has become an international symbol for the Hoosier capital and was initially designed to honor Civil War veterans from Indiana. From 1888 to 1901, this monument was built at the city's heart, the center of Circle Street (renamed Monument Circle in 1917), after a crusade by the state's most famous Civil War veterans, including Colonel Eli Lilly and General Lew Wallace. In this image, circa 1893, buildings surrounding the monument are draped with flags and bunting for a city celebration. German architect Bruno Schmitz won an international competition to design the monument, which was dedicated at a gala in 1902. Nearly 75 percent of Hoosier men of military age served in the Union army, a higher percentage than any other state except Delaware.

RIGHT: Having endured more than a hundred years of celebrations and hardships in the city that surrounds it, the Soldiers' and Sailors' Monument today stands as a tribute to the valor of Hoosier men and women who served in all of the nineteenth-century wars. The monument is built of gray limestone from the quarries in Owen County, Indiana. Its height from street level to the Lady Victory statue on top is 284 feet and six inches, making the Soldiers' and Sailors' Monument just seventeen feet shorter than the Statue of Liberty. The monument was designed so it could be integrated into the Circle, with fountains, pools, and terraced steps. In 1999, the Colonel Eli Lilly Civil War Museum opened in the monument's basement.

c. 1855

ISAAC COE'S HOUSE / COLUMBIA CLUB

A home on the Circle for the town's second doctor

ABOVE: Before construction of the Soldiers' and Sailors' Monument, the circular street at the heart of the city—now known as Monument Circle—was the address for several private homes. They included the residence of Dr. Isaac Coe (1782–1855), who became the second physician in Indianapolis when he moved here in 1821, just in time to treat victims of a malaria epidemic that hit the brand new city. Dr. Coe's house, as seen in this image from the 1850s, was on the northeast quadrant of what was then called Circle Street. For most of the 1800s, the Circle was a mix of residential and religious structures. Four churches had been built on Circle Street by 1843, including the First Presbyterian Church, where Dr. Coe served as an elder. Coe's office is visible to the left of his house in this photo.

ABOVE: Coe's home was replaced by a house that became offices for the Harrison Marching Club, formed in 1888 to help elect Benjamin Harrison as president. In 1900, the group, by then known as the Columbia Club, constructed this six-story structure.

RIGHT: One of the most prestigious private clubs in Indianapolis, the Columbia Club opened its current building in 1925. The ten-story building has banquet rooms, a fitness center, a library and overnight guest rooms. The Columbia Club quickly gained a reputation as a bastion for influential Republicans. Meanwhile, members of the rival Indianapolis Athletic Club, who met in a clubhouse at Meridian and Vermont Streets, were generally perceived as Democrats. In 2004, the Athletic Club closed, its clubhouse was converted into condos, and many members joined the Columbia Club, which had shed its partisan identification. A gathering spot for a range of Hoosier business and civic leaders, the Columbia Club typically houses more than 50 state legislators from across Indiana when the General Assembly is in session.

1917

CIRCLE THEATRE

Terra-cotta showcase for movies and later the Indianapolis Symphony Orchestra

LEFT: During the early 1900s, movies in Indianapolis were shown primarily on storefronts. In 1916, though, the lavish Circle Theatre opened in the southeast quadrant of Monument Circle as one of the first motion picture palaces in the Midwest. Indeed, the neoclassical-revival building became one of the first theaters west of New York built specifically to show movies. For sixty-five years, the terra-cotta Circle Theatre with its marquee of classical ornamental friezes—as seen in this photo from 1917—primarily showed movies, with occasional concerts by the likes of Frank Sinatra and jazz legend Dizzy Gillespie. However, with the proliferation of multiscreen cinemas in suburban malls during the 1960s, the once-elegant Circle Theatre began showing second-rate movies and slid into seediness.

ABOVE: The Circle Theatre—now the Hilbert Circle Theatre—had a $6.8 million renovation in 1984. The historic theater's stage was reconfigured and enlarged to accommodate the Indianapolis Symphony Orchestra, which made the renovated theater its home. The renovation included everything from restoration of the theater's seats to replacement of storefronts and playbill cases. In 1991, actress Kitty Carlisle hosted a centennial celebration of the birth of composer Cole Porter, a native Hoosier. Five years later, Indiana residents Stephen and Tomisue Hilbert donated $10 million to the symphony, resulting in the renaming of the concert hall as the Hilbert Circle Theatre. Occasionally, the theater reverts to its original use as a movie palace; it hosted the world premiere of *Hoosiers* in 1986.

c. 1925

ENGLISH HOTEL AND OPERA HOUSE / ANTHEM

A grand theater lost to the wrecking ball

1949

ABOVE: After nearly seventy years of continuous use, the English Hotel was razed, amid an outcry, in 1948. Deterioration, changing tastes, and the desire to showcase modern architecture all contributed to this decision. This July 26, 1949 photograph looks southeast toward the Monument and shows the remains of the brick foundation.

LEFT: For decades, the stunning English Hotel and Opera House dominated the northwest quadrant of Monument Circle. The majestic buildings, as seen in this photo from about 1925, were created by William H. English, a Democratic congressman and one of the city's first millionaires. The four-story opera house opened in 1880 and impressed the public with its frescoed walls and ceiling, massive pillars, elaborate chandeliers, and exterior balcony. With the largest stage in the city and plush red seats, the opera house presented opera, ballet, musicals, and lectures. Legendary performers such as Sarah Bernhardt and the Barrymores captivated audiences at the opera house, a showplace of the Midwest. After William English died in 1896, his son oversaw the completion of the hotel's second section, which stretched to Market Street.

ABOVE: This quadrant of the Circle has had several renovations and occupants since the English Hotel and Opera House was demolished. The hotel and opera house gave way to a building that was leased to the J. C. Penney chain, which opened a department store there in 1950. The J. C. Penney store remained on the Circle for almost thirty years, when downtown decline resulted in the store's closure. The prized location on Monument Circle once enjoyed by the English Hotel and Opera House is today the site of an office complex that includes Anthem Inc., an Indiana-based health benefits provider. The complex also houses a FedEx office.

PYLE HOUSE AND CHRIST CHURCH / CHASE TOWER

The site of a former hotel is now home to the state's tallest skyscraper

c. 1900

LEFT: The Pyle House, seen on the left, was a sleepy-looking boardinghouse on the southeast corner of Meridian and Ohio Streets that was torn down in 1905. The Christ Church Cathedral is visible in the photo to the right of the Pyle House. The cathedral, with its entrance on Monument Circle, was constructed between 1858 and 1861 and is the oldest religious structure in downtown Indianapolis; the Episcopal congregation's roots extend even further back to its original cathedral, which was built in 1837. Designed in the English Gothic style, Christ Church Cathedral is renowned for its choirs and support of the arts.

BELOW: Next to the eternal Christ Church Cathedral is the base of the forty-eight-story Chase Tower, the tallest building in the state of Indiana (pictured left). The downtown Chase complex houses an investment firm on its ground level. Known as the Bank One Tower when it opened in 1990 amid a series of mergers and acquisitions in the banking industry, the Chase Tower also houses law offices. Before the tower and its antennae changed the Indianapolis skyline, the state's tallest building was the thirty-eight-story One American Tower (initially the American United Life Tower) constructed in 1981.

1857

GOTT & FEATHERSTON,

DAGUERREOTYPE OF PENNSYLVANIA STREET

One of the earliest-known photographs of Indianapolis

LEFT: This 1857 scene is one of the oldest known streetscape photos of Indianapolis. The downtown scene depicts North Pennsylvania Street—still a dirt road—looking northward from East Washington Street. The building in the lower left was an auction house. In the upper right is Roberts Park United Methodist Church (then known as Roberts Chapel) in its original location at Pennsylvania and Market streets; the church had just installed its clock tower. The bell in the tower, in addition to calling the congregation to worship, served as the city's fire bell. In the southeast (right) corner, houses are being demolished for construction of the U.S. Post Office. In 1858, the population of Indianapolis, which was undergoing rapid growth, was nearly 18,000, compared to just 2,692 in 1840.

ABOVE: With rejuvenation continually underway today, downtown—as seen from the vantage point of Pennsylvania and Washington Streets—is the center of a metro area of more than 1.9 million people. Nearly one-fourth of all Hoosiers now live in the Indy metro area. The population of consolidated Indianapolis (Marion County) is 848,780, making it the twelfth-largest city in the country. The view up Pennsylvania takes in several bank towers and various buildings that are being redeveloped. The fourteen-story tower on the right, long known as the Consolidated Building, opened in 1913. Beginning in the 1990s, it sat vacant for nearly twenty years and fell into disrepair After an extensive renovation, the building reopened in 2015 as the Penn Street Tower with ninety-eight apartments, many with a view of the downtown skyline.

1905

BATES BLOCK: THE WHEN

A majestic Second Empire building

1907

LEFT: "WHEN is the store going to open?" That was the "teaser" promotional campaign for a clothing store preparing to open in the new Bates Block in 1875. A flamboyant personality, store owner John Brush didn't stop there. He also rented roofs of barns across Indiana and had "WHEN?" painted on them. The gimmick proved so successful that the Bates Block at 36 North Pennsylvania Street became known as the When Building and the emporium as the When Store. Shrewdly, Brush had capitalized on his major frustration: the uncertain opening of the store was due to needless delays. The When Building, seen here in a 1905 photo, had a mansard roof and an interior courtyard. The building was remodeled in the 1940s, when the balconies and balustrades lining the rooftop were eliminated.

RIGHT: The When Building was renamed the Ober Building and then demolished in 1995. The block of North Pennsylvania Street today has a mix of uses, including office towers for banks on the east (right) side of the street and a barbeque restaurant on the lower level of a multi-story parking garage on the west (left) side. City planners encourage developers of new downtown parking garages to create "pedestrian friendly" businesses on the sidewalk level such as cafes and retail outlets so that downtown workers and visitors don't stare at garage doors or rows of parked cars. The former American Fletcher National Bank Tower, to the right of the parking garage, was converted into a hotel. The Hilton Garden Inn opened in 2005 and has 188 rooms.

c. 1907

TRACTION TERMINAL / HILTON HOTEL
The country's largest interurban station

c. 1900

ABOVE: The northwest corner of Market and Illinois Streets has had several vital "lives" in Indianapolis history. In 1888, it became the site of the dome-shaped Cyclorama, shown here about 1900. The exhibition hall showcased a gigantic mural of the Civil War *Battle of Atlanta.*

LEFT: The Cyclorama was razed in 1903 for construction of the massive Indianapolis Traction Terminal, the hub of the state's popular interurban (electric rail) system. The nine-story Traction Terminal with adjacent train shed was touted as the largest in the world when it opened on September 12, 1904. Passengers rode the interurbans, which were electric rail cars, on lines to and from smaller cities such as Fort Wayne, Terre Haute, and Franklin. Next to the terminal was the nine-track train shed.

RIGHT: By the late 1930s, most interurban lines had been discontinued, and many tracks were paved for use by buses. The terminal building became a hub for bus operations before being demolished in 1972, four years after the old train shed also was torn down. For many years, the site was occupied by an office tower for Blue Cross-Blue Shield of Indianapolis. More recently, the site at 120 West Market has been the setting for hotels and restaurants. In 2006, the Hilton Hotel & Suites opened with 332 guest rooms as part of a downtown hotel boom; Hilton alone has five properties in the Mile Square. Adjacent to the hotel is McCormick & Schmick's, a seafood restaurant.

1911

WILLIAM H. BLOCK COMPANY
The former department store is now home to residential apartments

LEFT: An indefatigable immigrant from Hungary, William H. Block founded a department store that became a favorite for generations of Indianapolis residents. Block studied to be a rabbi in his homeland, then failed at several endeavors elsewhere in America, including farming and telegraphy, before he moved to the city in 1896. His legendary department store is seen here in 1911, the year of its grand opening on the southwest corner of Illinois and Market Streets. Known far and wide as Block's, but officially called the William H. Block Company, the store had previously operated for about fifteen years in a building on Washington Street. The eight-story Block store benefited from its location across from the bustling Traction Terminal.

ABOVE: More than 115 years after William H. Block showed up in Indianapolis with a dream, the building that housed his department store is still associated with retailing. A large clothing store is located on the first floor, and the upper floors of the former Block Building have been converted into residential units. Block, who became a benefactor of the Riley Hospital for Children and various charities, died in 1928. His sons oversaw expansion of the department store, opening Block outlets in shopping centers in suburbs such as Glendale. A series of ownership changes, though, meant that in 1988 all of the Block stores in Indiana became part of the Cincinnati-based Lazarus chain. Lazarus closed the flagship Block store in 1993, opening the door for today's retailers, including the T. J. Maxx store seen here.

25

1926

WASHINGTON STREET

The city's major commercial street is also known as the National Road

ABOVE: During the yuletide season of 1926, the view looking west along Washington Street takes in various department stores, including the flagship of arguably the most beloved of all Indianapolis-based retailers, L. S. Ayres & Co. The store was founded by local merchant Lyman S. Ayres (1824–96), whose son, Frederick, assumed control after his father's death. The westward view down Washington Street also takes in part of the grand Lincoln Hotel. The streetcar tracks and the broad width of Washington shows it was designed to be the city's main east-west artery. Although the street's width hasn't changed, L. S. Ayres has undergone several transformations. The chain was purchased in 1986 by St. Louis–based May Department Stores Company. Seven years later, the company announced Ayres would not be part of the Circle Centre Mall and closed the downtown store.

ABOVE: The glass-enclosed Artsgarden spanning Washington Street is the most striking symbol of Circle Centre, the $307 million retail and entertainment complex that's among the crown jewels of downtown rejuvenation. Circle Centre, which features 130 retailers, restaurants, bistros, and bars, opened in 1995 and was developed by Indianapolis-based Simon Property Group, the country's largest owner of shopping malls. However, the Artsgarden is owned and operated by the Arts Council of Indianapolis, a private, non-profit group. Seven stories tall with a large atrium, the Artsgarden serves as an elegant setting for receptions and exhibits. It stretches across Washington at its intersection with Illinois Street. In 2014, *The Indianapolis Star* moved into Circle Centre and sold its long-time office building on North Pennsylvania Street

1922

LINCOLN HOTEL / PNC CENTER

This flat-iron hotel was the state's first demolition by implosion

LEFT: Hoosiers have always felt they had a special relationship with Abraham Lincoln, who lived in southern Indiana from when he was seven until he was twenty-one; the distinctive, flatiron Lincoln Hotel was one of many buildings and businesses named in honor of "the Great Emancipator." The hotel opened in 1918—four years before this photo was taken—at the corner of West Washington Street and Kentucky Avenue. It quickly became the setting for political, civic, and social gatherings, as did the rival Claypool Hotel. The posh Claypool, which opened in 1903 at Illinois and Washington Streets, was built on the site of the legendary Bates House, where Abraham Lincoln spoke from a balcony to a crowd of Hoosiers in 1861. During his White House years, Lincoln said, "I grew up in Indiana"—even though many Americans associate him exclusively with Kentucky and Illinois. The Indianapolis hotel named in his honor closed in 1970 and was imploded three years later.

1865

RIGHT: Among the first modern, urban hotels built in Indianapolis was the Hyatt Regency Hotel, which opened in 1977 on the former Lincoln Hotel site. The Hyatt is part of a complex known as the PNC Center; by the time of its construction, most of the grand hotels of the early 20th century were gone. The Claypool Hotel, where celebrity guests ranged from Eleanor Roosevelt to Gene Autry, closed after a fire in 1967. This photo of the Hyatt was taken from the ninth floor of Embassy Suites, which is on the former Claypool site. With about 500 rooms and dazzling glass elevators, the Hyatt Regency has a twenty-story atrium, a bank, and several restaurants, including a rooftop dining spot that revolves. Because the Hyatt is near the city's sports arenas, the hotel is a favorite of visiting spectators at NFL and NBA games.

LEFT: Due to the heavy rain on April 30, 1865, when Lincoln's body lay in state in the Indiana Statehouse, historians believe this photograph of Lincoln's Indianapolis hearse was staged in the days before or following. Here it is posed in front of the Commercial House, later the site of the Lincoln Hotel. Four years earlier, several of these horses had pulled Lincoln's carriage when he visited Indianapolis.

PUBLIC COMFORT STATION / ARTSGARDEN
Classical underground restrooms for the general public

BELOW: The "comfort stations"—one serving female pedestrians, with an adjacent one for males—provided a basic service in 1911, when this photo was taken. Then only one year old, the comfort stations were belowground public restrooms built for $17,000 on an island at the intersection of Kentucky Avenue and West Washington Street. The city council prohibited shoeshine stands at the comfort stations because they might encourage loafing. Within six months of the stations' opening, women's groups were expressing concerns about their sanitary conditions and lack of ventilation. Even so, the comfort stations were used for decades, particularly by early- and late-shift workers who could not use the facilities in department stores and office buildings.

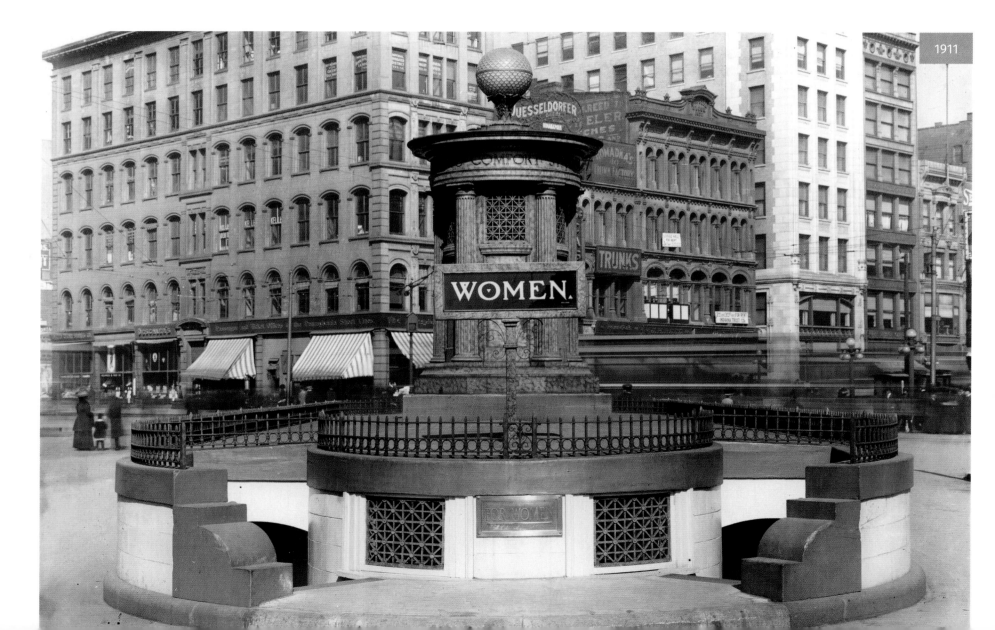

1911

BELOW: Over the years, concerns about safety in the comfort stations increased. They were sealed off in 1963. The view at the long-gone comfort stations site includes the above-ground Artsgarden, the symbol for Circle Centre mall; part of the office wing of PNC Center, and such historic storefronts as the former Goodman Jewelry store and

two neighboring buildings, all of which date to the 1890s. The three structures now are part of a retail and office complex with upper-level apartments. They adjoin the Conrad Hotel, a luxury hotel that opened in 2006 and has spacious, penthouse condos.

1935

CAPITOL AND INDIANA THEATERS

A corner known for entertainment since the 1850s

ABOVE: Although they existed side by side when this photo was taken in 1935, the Indiana Theatre and the Capitol Theatre had vastly different histories and would have far different fates. The Spanish Baroque–style Indiana Theatre, built as a movie palace, was only two years old when this photograph was taken. The auditorium of 3,200 seats made it the largest cinema constructed in the city at the time. In contrast, the Capitol Theatre had been built at Washington Street and Capitol Avenue way back in 1858. Known then as the Metropolitan, it was a favorite venue for circuses and vaudeville. It was from the Metropolitan

stage in 1861 that a local military veteran announced the grim news that the Civil War had broken out. The Metropolitan later became the Park before another name change to the Capitol. Stock companies performed comedies and melodramas there, although it also began showing movies after being renamed the Capitol Theatre.

RIGHT: Cinerama, the motion picture system that kicked off the wide-screen trend, premiered at the Indiana Theatre in September 1960. Audiences in the revitalized theater were captivated by the extra-wide image projected onto a curved screen.

1960

ABOVE: As majestic as ever, the terra-cotta Indiana Theatre today is the home of the Indiana Repertory Theatre, a professional equity theater that presents plays ranging from British classics to world premieres by American playwrights. As a movie theater, the Indiana became the first in the state with Panavision, 3-D capabilities, and stereophonic sound. Even so, the Indiana Theatre was slated for demolition before it underwent a $5 million renovation so the acclaimed Indiana Repertory Theatre could move in. The six-story theater now has three auditoriums, including the 600-seat Mainstage Theatre. On the top floor is the Indiana Roof Ballroom, which features a deep blue ceiling of twinkling "stars." The Capitol closed in 1935; an office tower has occupied the site since 1982. Today it houses a teachers' credit union, a school board association, and some departments of state government.

c. 1865

MASONIC HALL AND STORES / SIMON HEADQUARTERS

Birthplace of Indiana's second constitution

LEFT: In 1851, Masonic Hall (far right) was only a year old on the southeast corner of Capitol Avenue (then Tennessee Street) and West Washington Street when it served as the site of Indiana's second constitutional convention. Debate was limited to the daytime hours because the hall, with its gas-lit chandeliers and chairs of red upholstery, was double-booked—at night, there were theatrical and musical performances by a touring company. The opening of Masonic Hall, shown here in the 1860s, enhanced the city's sophistication as a venue for opera concerts. Next to Masonic Hall was a German-owned furniture store, Spiegel, Thoms & Co.; it was one of an astonishing ninety-one German-American businesses that were flourishing in the vicinity by 1875. By the turn of the nineteenth century, almost seventy percent of the city's population was of German ancestry.

ABOVE: Clearly visible from the former site of Masonic Hall are the glass and limestone headquarters of Simon Property Group, the light granite Westin Hotel, and (far right) the distinctively blue J. W. Marriott Hotel. Opened in 2011 as the world's largest Marriott with more than 1,000 guest rooms, the 33-story hotel was touted as a factor in Indy's selection as the host of the 2012 Super Bowl. Both the Marriott and the Westin are connected by covered walkways to the Indiana Convention Center. Simon Property Group, the world's largest developer of shopping malls, moved into its headquarters in 2006. The towering hotels and corporate headquarters replaced the long-gone, family-owned German businesses. Today, about seventeen percent of Indianapolis residents identify themselves as having German heritage, a shift that reflects the increasing percentage of Hispanics, African Americans, and other ethnic groups in the city.

1937

CADLE TABERNACLE / FIREHOUSE SQUARE
Public hall for everything from graduations to Klan rallies

LEFT: The Cadle Tabernacle, shown here in the 1930s, hosted a variety of public events, including religious revivals, teachers' conventions, and dance marathons. A Spanish-style convention center and revival house with a whitewashed facade, the tabernacle was built in 1921 on the northwest corner of Ohio and New Jersey Streets. The owner, entrepreneur E. Howard Cadle, intended for the tabernacle to be used to promote nondenominational Christianity, but the building's use expanded to hundreds of secular gatherings. In the 1920s, when the Ku Klux Klan dominated Hoosier politics, several of its rallies were at the tabernacle.

ABOVE: The Cadle Tabernacle was demolished in the late 1960s to create parking lots for banks and other businesses east of Monument Circle. Before and after the implosion of Market Square Arena in 2001, upscale housing was developed in the blocks surrounding the arena, including the former Cadle Tabernacle site. Town houses and condominiums are springing up as part of the downtown rejuvenation and resulting clamor for luxury urban living. In 1999, the Firehouse Square condo complex (shown here) opened on the Cadle Tabernacle site with a waiting list of 500 buyers for the fifty-six units. A similar residential boom of condos and apartments has been underway across downtown.

c. 1904

MARION COUNTY COURTHOUSE / CITY-COUNTY BUILDING
An architectural gem lost to the wrecking ball before the preservation movement took hold

LEFT: The architectural jewels in most of Indiana's ninety-two counties are the courthouses, many built in the 1800s. Many small Hoosier cities designed their town squares around their courthouses. With its circular center, Indianapolis didn't do that, but for eighty-five years the ornate Marion County Courthouse remained in use. Designed in the Second Empire style with a ninety-seven foot tower and clock, the courthouse cost $1.4 million when built in 1876 on East Washington Street. Several city government offices were located in the Marion County Courthouse (seen here around 1904) until 1909, when the first Indianapolis City Hall was built amid much hoopla at Ohio and Alabama streets. By the 1960s, both the courthouse and city hall were considered outdated and inadequate for their purposes. The city hall building was used as the home of the Indiana State Museum until 2002. The decaying Marion County Courthouse was torn down in the early 1960s.

RIGHT: A twenty-eight-story, starkly rectangular structure, the City-County Building serves for many Hoosiers as the symbol of Unigov, even though the office tower was built almost eight years before the pioneering merger of city and county governments. Offices for the mayor and workers for city as well as county governments are housed in the building, which opened in 1962 on the former courthouse site. Championed by Indianapolis Mayor Richard Lugar in the late 1960s, Unigov consolidated local governments, stretching the newly merged city from eighty-two to 402 square miles. As a result, the city's population almost doubled, jumping from 480,000 to 740,000. The new twenty-nine-member city council had its first meeting in the City-County Building in 1971, a year after Unigov became effective. The mayor's office is on the top floor of the tower.

VANCE BLOCK / ZIPPER BUILDING

Two unique structures which were appreciated too late

LEFT: This 1893 photograph shows the majestic Vance Block building, a flatiron structure at the intersection of South Pennsylvania Street, Virginia Avenue, and East Washington Street. Mary J. (Bates) Vance, widow of merchant Lawrence Vance, built the structure in 1876. Her money and entrepreneurial spirit likely came from her father, Hervey Bates, who was Marion County's first sheriff. The Vance Block housed a range of businesses, including a bank, a savings and loan, architects, and a business college. The building is decorated in this photo for a Grand Army of the Republic encampment, a Civil War reunion. Within a few years the tower was removed to make way for two additional floors and became known as the Indiana Trust Building.

BELOW: It's easy to see why the "Zipper Building" was the widespread nickname for the office structure at the intersection. The Zipper Building, which housed a bank, advertising agency, and other offices, was an example of the International style of modern architecture popular when it opened in 1959. This design approach rebelled against historic architectural styles; in the case of the Zipper Building and other boldly designed structures, the goal was to create a building that would be distinct from its environment.

ABOVE: The structure at the intersection was completely remodeled in 2007. Now known as the Broadbent Building and named after a realty company, it houses offices and Fogo de Chao, a Brazilian steakhouse. The restaurant immediately became popular with, among others, Indy 500 drivers from South America, including three-time winner Helio Castroneves. The redesign of the building, though, has received mixed reviews, as did the distinctive, so-called "Zipper Building". One aspect remains from the long-ago Vance Block building: A massive safe in the basement.

1916

JAMES WHITCOMB RILEY HOME

A Victorian gem preserved to the Hoosier Poet's era

LEFT: Many called him "the Hoosier Poet." Certainly, James Whitcomb Riley was Indiana's best-known poet. Beloved for his poems celebrating rural life and the joys of childhood such as swimming holes, bullfrogs, and jack-o'-lanterns, Riley was born in 1849 in Greenfield, east of Indianapolis. For about thirty years, he lived in this house in the Lockerbie neighborhood. A masterful entertainer who elicited hoots, cheers, and stomps from audiences when he read his poems in Hoosier dialect, Riley was invited to perform at the White House and became wealthy as a result of cross-country tours. He had written more than 1,900 poems, including *The Raggedy Man* and *Little Orphant Annie*, by the time he died in this house in 1916. After his funeral, more than 35,000 mourners filed by his casket when it lay in state in the rotunda of the Indiana Statehouse.

ABOVE: The elegant Italianate home where James Whitcomb Riley lived during his years as the biggest celebrity in Indianapolis is now a house museum. Interestingly, Riley never owned the home, even though experts say he made more money from his poetry than any other American poet, including Robert Frost and Carl Sandburg. Instead of becoming a homeowner with the demands of his tour itinerary, Riley, a bachelor, preferred to be a permanent "paying guest" in the house of friends at 528 Lockerbie Street, living amid a cozy family atmosphere during breaks in his schedule. After his death, several of his friends established the acclaimed Riley Hospital for Children in Indianapolis as a tribute to the poet.

c. 1975

LOCKERBIE SQUARE

Downtown's oldest and most intact preservation district

ABOVE: Lockerbie Square, one of Indianapolis's oldest neighborhoods, dates to the 1830s. Early settlers Thomas and Janet McQuat developed the neighborhood at this time, which is less than one mile—a brisk walk—east of Monument Circle. The McQuats named Lockerbie Street in honor of Janet's father, Scottish immigrant George Murray Lockerbie. The neighborhood became popular for a mix of uses, from the homes of celebrities such as poet James Whitcomb Riley to workers' cottages, a general store,

and a doctor's office. However, Lockerbie's charm for many Hoosiers had diminished by the mid-1930s. This photo shows the deterioration of cottages on the 400 block of North Park Avenue, startling to those who know the neighborhood now as an area of historic restoration. The cottage on the right was built around 1860; it was the home of Herman Lieber, a businessman and arts patron.

ABOVE: With its white picket fences, cobblestone streets, and restored historic homes, Lockerbie Square is a source of civic pride and continually visited by tourists. Unlike many Midwestern cities, where much of the nineteenth-century downtown housing stock was demolished, the Lockerbie cottages endured despite economic reversals and shifts in popular taste. Amid the towering trees, pedestrians on Lockerbie's bricked sidewalks can almost forget they are in a modern city—even though nearby office towers are visible from many vantage points. Spearheaded by Indiana Landmarks, major restoration of Lockerbie's private homes picked up steam once the neighborhood was added to the National Register of Historic Places in 1973. With one of the city's strongest neighborhood groups, Lockerbie residents host popular home tours and a Fourth of July celebration.

1888

HAMMOND BLOCK

A preservation success at the gateway to Massachusetts Avenue

ABOVE: This Italianate building with six chimneys at 310 Massachusetts Avenue has been everything from a doctor's house to law offices, a saloon, a Chinese laundry, and a college for surgeons. Known as the Hammond Block Building when it was constructed in 1874, the brick structure was designed as a flatiron, a term used to describe the shape buildings took to fit odd-sized lots such as this location on the diagonal, three-way intersection of Massachusetts, Delaware, and New York Streets. In the 1870s and 1880s, the building was a physician's office and residence. From 1887 to 1891, the Central College of Physicians and Surgeons conducted classes on the second and third floors; cadavers and all kinds of medical equipment were kept here. The college, a forerunner to the Indiana University School of Medicine, was using the building when this photo was taken in 1888.

1977

ABOVE: In 1945 Joe Budnick planned to open a liquor store in the aging building, but could not acquire a liquor license due to its proximity to churches. Instead, he opened a fishing supply store that operated on this site until the 1970s.

ABOVE: Considered inefficient because their design resulted in odd-shaped rooms, many flatiron buildings were demolished in the mid-twentieth century. The Hammond Block was slated for the wrecking ball in 1979 when local attorney Henry Price decided to save it. After the renovation initiated by Price, the renamed Price Hammond Block became law offices. In 2009, Three Mass Condos, a ship-like, ten-story building of luxury condos with terraces, was constructed to the north of the flatiron building. The three-piece sculpture seen on the left, titled Viewfinders, was created by Indianapolis artist Eric Nordgulen in 1996; it serves as the gateway to today's dynamic Massachusetts Avenue arts and cultural district.

c. 1896

DAS DEUTSCHE HAUS / ATHENAEUM

German clubhouse still known for fitness, entertainment, and beer

ABOVE: The German cultural center was known as Das Deutsche Haus in the 1890s when the distinctive landmark was completed in two phases at the three-way corner of Michigan Street, New Jersey Street, and Massachusetts Avenue. Designed by architects Bernard Vonnegut and Arthur Bohn, the structure, seen in this photo from circa 1896, has steeped gables, stained glass windows, and a massive, pitched roof. The expansive structure featured a turnverein (athletic or gymnastics club), a biergarten (beer garden), and the Rathskeller, a German restaurant that has endured as the city's oldest dining spot. The Das Deutsche Haus name, though, did not endure. Because of anti-German sentiment following World War I, the cultural center was given a Greek name, the Athenaeum.

ABOVE: During visits by internationally acclaimed novelist Kurt Vonnegut to his hometown before his death in 2007, he often referred to the Athenaeum at 401 East Michigan Street as his grandfather's "masterpiece." The Athenaeum was spared from possible demolition (it had significantly deteriorated by the 1980s) thanks to a city-wide fund-raising effort that included two volunteers who raised pledges by sleeping on its roof. The biergarten has become a popular venue for concerts and events such as German heritage festivals. In addition to a theater and the Rathskeller, the Athenaeum today includes a YMCA and banquet rooms, one of them called the Vonnegut Room. Considered among the classic examples of German Renaissance Revival architecture in the country, the Athenaeum is listed on the National Register of Historic Places.

BUSCHMANN BLOCK

A mixed-use Italianate building still serves the St. Joseph neighborhood

BELOW: A Prussian immigrant who came to Indianapolis in 1852, William Buschmann settled in the St. Joseph neighborhood just as the city was expanding northward from its original Mile Square boundary at North Street. A savvy entrepreneur, Buschmann decided the neighborhood, a mixed-use community of row houses and retail shops, was ripe with opportunity. In 1871 he erected the first portion of the Buschmann Block, an L-shaped, three-story building with seven bays on the 900 block of Fort Wayne

Avenue. Buschmann ran successful grocery and dry goods operations in his namesake building. Upper floors were used as residences for the extended Buschmann family. At some point after 1895, the upper floors were converted for warehouse use. But the St. Joseph neighborhood—a triangular area of about fourteen blocks—struggled after the 1930s. In 1939, the grocery shut down.

c. 1890

BELOW: Life has come full circle for many structures in the triangular-shaped St. Joseph neighborhood, including the Buschmann Block. Regarded as one of the few large Italianate commercial buildings left in Indianapolis, the Buschmann has a decidedly mixed use today that reflects its beginnings in the 1800s: retail stores on the first floor and residences on the upper floors. Businesses at the sidewalk level include a fitness studio. The upper floors of the Buschmann Block have been rehabilitated to about a dozen apartments. The restoration of the Buschmann Block, which today is listed on the National Register of Historic Places, is a sterling example of efforts underway in St. Joseph, which has become a hot spot again.

MASSACHUSETTS AVENUE

Stout's shoe store spans a century of retailing on "Mass Ave"

LEFT: During the 1870s, the 300, 400, and 500 blocks of Massachusetts Avenue were developed as a new retail district. Although shopping along "Mass Ave" never had the prestige enjoyed by the merchants on the Circle or Washington Street, the area in the northeast part of the Mile Square experienced solid retail and commercial success. Early merchants included Harry Stout, who opened this small shoe store at 318 Massachusetts Avenue. Almost from the beginning, Stout's Shoes specialized in hard-to-find sizes. Stout's was located just south of Marott's Department Store, which promoted itself as "the holiday department store of 1910," one year after this photo was taken. The store's owner, English merchant George Marott, had also started in the shoe business; by 1910, his wealth was estimated at more than $2 million.

ABOVE: The Massachusetts Avenue of the twenty-first century enjoys as much bustle as it did in the nineteenth, but it is now bustling with an artistic edge and with culinary delights. With the Theatre on the Square, arts galleries, sculptures and other public artwork, and the nearby American Cabaret Theatre, Mass Ave is considered to be the center of a downtown arts district. Upscale and ethnic restaurants have flourished since the 1990s and nearby are renovated buildings such as the Real Silk condominiums, which once housed a parachute and women's silk hose factory. Nightclubs along Mass Ave include the Chatterbox, a tavern known for its year-round Christmas lights, jazz music, and Jamaican patties. Although the five-story Marott's Department Store is now the Marott Center health care offices, one neighborhood landmark is unchanged—Stout's Shoes remains.

1925

POLK'S SANITARY MILK COMPANY
Giant milk bottles advertised this building's purpose

ABOVE: The corners of Polk's Sanitary Milk Company building were shaped like giant milk bottles. This photo was taken in 1925, fifteen years after the dairy was built on the northeast corner of Fifteenth and Lewis Streets. The company was founded in 1893 by Greenwood resident James Polk, a Civil War veteran. The company's slogan, "Polk's milk—always ahead," was framed around a cow's head. Contractors had told Polk's son-in-law that dairy bottles could not be created as huge cornerstones. But Polk's son-in-law saw laborers building cisterns and asked them to construct the cisterns upside down and aboveground, and so the dairy ended up with its giant replicas of milk bottles. Polk became the state's largest milk company, but it began experiencing financial problems in the 1950s because of competition from large food chains.

ABOVE: Decorated with a vivid mural, a maintenance building for Indianapolis Public Schools sits just north of the former Polk's site. As the state's largest school district, IPS educates about 40,000 students. The unique bottling plant—with skylights that illuminated the interior's vast bottling room—met the wrecking ball in the 1960s. The dairy's stables still stand, though. The old stables, where Polk kept the delivery horses, are located just south of Sixteenth Street on Lewis Street. The former stable building is part of the IPS maintenance complex. IPS, which has boundaries roughly conforming to the pre-Unigov city limits, is one of eleven public school districts in Marion County.

1864

CAMP MORTON

In 1864 the state fairgrounds had a different purpose

ABOVE AND RIGHT: With the outbreak of the Civil War, Governor Oliver P. Morton decided that the new Indiana State Fairgrounds north of the Mile Square would be the best site for the induction and training of Union army soldiers. Thus, Camp Morton was born near Twentieth and Alabama Streets. It primarily became a prisoner-of-war camp, as seen in this photo from 1864. After Morton promised President Lincoln that Indiana would provide 10,000 troops, animal stalls were converted into barracks. By the time recruits poured in, tents, guardhouses, and a hospital had been erected. By the end of the war, 15,000 Confederate soldiers had been imprisoned at Camp Morton, with a peak of 5,000 in July 1864. After the war, the State Fair once again returned to the site.

1864

ABOVE: Queen Anne–style houses and other elegant residences were built during the late 1800s and early 1900s on the site of the former Camp Morton. The genteel neighborhood also became the home of Indiana's top art school, the John Herron School of Art. Although all appears to be unchanged today from 1910, the Herron-Morton neighborhood deteriorated dramatically beginning in the 1930s as affluent residents moved northward. Several spacious homes became apartment houses and the crime rates increased. Restoration of Herron-Morton Place kicked off in the 1970s, and by 1983 it was listed in the National Register of Historic Places. In addition to Queen Anne–style homes, the neighborhood features houses of Italianate and Tudor Revival architecture.

1926

TALBOTT STREET THEATRE
The neighborhood theater lives on, hosting movies, dinner theater, and a gay club

LEFT: The Talbott Street Theatre opened as a movie house in 1920. But the building (seen here in 1926) would become far better known in other ways during the decades to come, as would four blocks of Talbott Avenue. During the mid-1950s, the art festival that would become one of the city's oldest was established: the Talbott Street Art Fair. It began modestly in an alley as a way for students at the nearby John Herron School of Art to sell their creations in June at the end of the semester. During the 1960s, the Talbott area became associated with peace activists and bohemians, as well as artists. By then, the movie house had become the Black Curtain Dinner Theatre. Along with the adjacent Hummingbird Café, the dinner theater was popular through much of the 1970s.

ABOVE: Today the Talbott Street building is a gay nightclub that opened in the former theater at 2145 North Talbott Avenue in 2002, although the area has been known as a welcoming one for the gay community since the early 1980s. The current nightclub, which has a Studio 54–style dance floor, replaced other gay clubs on the same site. Meanwhile, the Talbott Street Art Fair exploded in popularity. Today hundreds of painters, potters, and other artists sell everything from ceramics and macramé wall hangings at the festival that invariably draws elbow-to-elbow crowds. Four blocks of Talbott Avenue are closed to traffic for the annual fair, which is now one of the largest in the city. And yes, the Talbott area is still considered a bit bohemian.

c. 1895

RUSKAUP BUILDING
An 1870s building in the heart of the Cottage Home neighborhood

c. 1900

ABOVE: The Ruskaup family's home adjacent to the store was completed in 1892 by the Indianapolis architectural firm of Vonnegut & Bohn. It was built for about $12,000 and includes parquet floors, five fireplaces, and carved woodwork.

LEFT: In a working-class neighborhood on the near Eastside, just west of the U.S. Arsenal, German immigrant Frederick Ruskaup opened a grocery and butcher shop in 1875. This photo of the Ruskaup Grocery in the 700 block of North Dorman Street was taken in the 1890s. The second floor of the grocery consisted of apartments known as the Ruskaup Flats. Three large, horse-drawn wagons made deliveries daily from the store. Ruskaup ran his grocery, bakery, and butcher shop in the building's northern half and the south half became a saloon patronized by the Irish and German residents of the neighborhood. After Prohibition, the tavern was replaced by Henry H. Luedemann's confectionary. Three generations of the Ruskaup family operated the grocery for over 75 years.

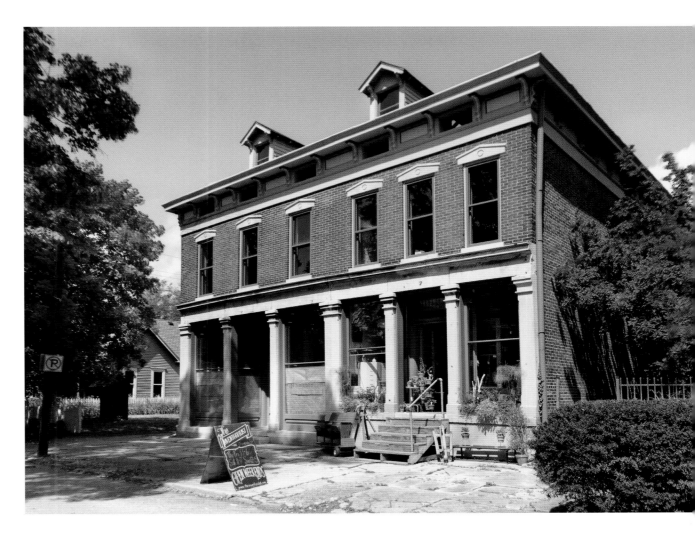

ABOVE: After the Ruskaups closed the business in the late 1950s, the building was used as a pool hall and storage for Hogue Construction and Cliff Mills Caulking. Windows were boarded up and the decorative brackets removed. After sitting vacant for over two decades, owners John Dugger and Becky Garland began restoration of the Cottage Home neighborhood building in 2007. Although the interior is not yet restored, the downstairs commercial space is once again occupied, giving neighbors a glimpse of how the building must have once been a hub and gathering place for local residents. Gordo's Fine Woodworking helped with the exterior restoration and never left, renting the northern half. In 2013, Kris Bowman opened The Inventorialist, a shop specializing in vintage, industrial, and designer-made goods.

c. 1885

CLIFFORD PLACE / TEACHERS' TREASURES
The grand Fletcher mansion later became a sanatorium

ABOVE: Known as "Clifford Place," the mansion of businessman Stoughton A. Fletcher was built in 1872 on East Tenth Street, then called Clifford Avenue. When Fletcher built Clifford Place, he was president of the Indianapolis Gas Company. In 1878, he became president of Atlas Engine Works, which reaped enormous success. He moved with his first wife, Ruth, and their four children into the grand Clifford Place, seen here in a photo from the 1880s. After Ruth Fletcher's death in 1889, her husband remarried but he also died here six years later. In the late 1890s neurologist Dr. Albert Sterne purchased it and the surrounding estate from the Fletcher family to create an exclusive private sanatorium for the treatment of mental disorders.

"THE NORWAY'S" DR. ALBERT E. STERNE'S SANATORIUM, INDIANAPOLIS, IND.

LEFT: The well-respected Norway's Sanatorium, named after the large Norway maples on the grounds, was the first mental institution in the state to employ insulin, metrazol, and electric shock therapy. The mansion-turned-sanatorium was demolished in 1957.

ABOVE: On the former site of the Fletcher family's mansion, Teachers' Treasures, a nonprofit group that provides free school supplies to teachers, has leased a former supermarket building since 2007. Kroger supermarkets chain had opened a grocery store that remained for nearly fifty years at 1800 E. Tenth Street. Today, the mural on the building's east wall depicts books, an apple, and other supplies cherished by teachers. At the opposite end of the former Kroger is Family Dollar, a discount store.

1905

WOODRUFF PLACE FOUNTAIN
Fountains enrich the park-like setting of the city's first planned suburb

c. 1970

c. 1970

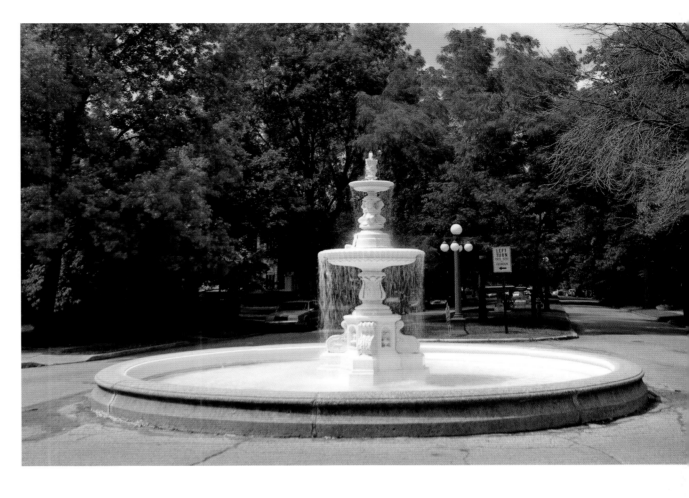

OPPOSITE AND LEFT: Indianapolis novelist Booth Tarkington used the Victorian-era homes of Woodruff Place as models for the spacious houses of the genteel aristocrats in his book *The Magnificent Ambersons*. This tree-lined subdivision was laid out in the early 1870s with three boulevards bisected by esplanades. Its developer, James O. Woodruff, oversaw the creation of statues cast in pot metal for the esplanades and elegant fountains, as seen in the main 1905 photo of Woodruff Place's Middle Drive. James Woodruff's goal was to create a retreat for cultured, affluent Hoosiers. Many of the 300 homes in Woodruff Place were built in the Edwardian and Queen Anne architectural styles.

ABOVE: During the first half of the twentieth century, some of the same homes had gradually declined as affluent residents moved to suburban neighborhoods. For some families, the Depression of the 1930s meant they could no longer afford the big houses. Many of the Woodruff Place homes were subdivided into apartments, while others became boardinghouses. In 1962, Indianapolis finally annexed Woodruff Place, which was struggling with serious decay. Renovation of the homes began in the 1970s. Many of the roomy Woodruff Place homes have been restored to their elegance of the late 1800s, and the neighborhood hosts one of the city's most popular yard sales each year.

1910

WONDERLAND AMUSEMENT PARK / P. R. MALLORY AND COMPANY

Visitors to Wonderland could witness the daring feat of "Queenie" the diving horse

ABOVE: Hundreds of carefree, stylishly dressed people were enjoying themselves in 1910 at Wonderland Amusement Park, a lavish entertainment area on the Eastside. The amusement park featured an artificial lake, diving horses (a mare named Queenie was a crowd favorite), a waterslide, a fun house, and landscaped gardens. The twenty-four buildings of Wonderland, which was at East Washington and Gray Streets, were designed in "dreamlike" architecture. When illuminated at night, the park's 125-foot central tower was visible for miles. More than 8,000 people attended the opening of Wonderland in 1906. Special

attractions at the park included bands, acrobats, and trick cyclists. Sadly, Wonderland's life was not wonderfully long. On a Sunday in 1911, the amusement park burned to the ground.

RIGHT: Prior to the amusement park, visitors were entertained at the East Washington Baseball Park, shown here in about 1904 looking northeast toward Washington and Gray Streets. In 1902 the Indianapolis Indians played their first season in this park, which was constructed on railroad-owned property in the winter of 1899. The Indians played three seasons here until moving to the new park on West Washington Street, which predated Bush Stadium and today's Victory Field.

ABOVE: Today the setting of the long-gone Wonderland Amusement Park is the site of the former plant of P. R. Mallory and Company, an Indianapolis-based electrical components manufacturer. The Englewood Community Development Corporation received a grant to stabilize and market neglected Mallory buildings. As part of the East Washington Street Partnership, the Englewood CDC is working with others to revitalize a four-mile section of the old National Road—one of Indianapolis's most important industrial and commercial corridors. Washington Street assets located between Interstate 65 and Sherman Drive include the old Ford factory, the East Washington Street Carnegie Library, and Willard Park.

c. 1935

THE BARGE

An old trolley car was transformed into a boat-themed drive-in

LEFT: The Barge, seen here around 1935, was a fish and chips eatery shaped like a boat. The restaurant had a gangplank, life preservers, and a roped deck. The "boat" itself was created from an old trolley car. Alas, the Barge, being located on dry land at East Washington and Denny Streets, didn't stay at this location for very long, and this site later housed an ice cream parlor in the late 1930s. The Barge, though, was a delightful example of a type of roadside architecture known as "mimetic," in which a building's design mimics the product or services it offers.

ABOVE: A used car dealership now sits on the former site of the Barge. This photo shows Denny Street from a vantage point just north of East Washington Street. A busy thoroughfare today, the street played an even more significant role in the 1800s and first half of the 1900s as the Indianapolis portion of the National Road. After the railroad boom of the 1850s, use of the National Road declined. It revived with the introduction of the car, then diminished again as a result of interstate highway construction in the 1970s. Some roadside businesses closed and were replaced by pawnshops, tobacco stores, and tanning salons. Today, though, groups concerned with the heritage of the National Road are mobilizing to beautify the areas alongside it.

c. 1908

IRVINGTON

This Methodist church was converted from a house in the historic neighborhood

ABOVE: The Eastside neighborhood of Irvington began as a suburban village during the 1870s and was annexed into the city in 1902. Named in honor of Washington Irving with several streets (such as Hawthorne and Emerson) also named after renowned authors, Irvington gained a reputation as a haven for literary and artistic types. Butler University (then Butler College) flourished for more than 40 years in the neighborhood until moving to the Northside in the 1920s. This spacious, Tudor Revival-style house was built in 1906 as the residence of Jacob Dorsey Forrest and his wife, Albertina, both of whom taught at Butler. In 1914, the college's president, Thomas Carr Howe, purchased the house at 9 North Audubon Road. This part of the street is unusual in that it loops around two, tree-lined circles.

ABOVE: Irvington United Methodist Church bought the historic house in 1924, constructed an addition, and today is known locally as the "church on the circle." As Irvington was developed during the first half of the twentieth century, bungalows and Sears "kit homes" were built. Together with the historic homes constructed in Second Empire and Queen Anne styles, the neighborhood has one of the most extensive ranges of houses in the city. Distinguished neighborhood residents have included Hoosier Group painter William Forsyth and cartoonist Kin Hubbard, whose "Abe Martin" character, a cracker barrel philosopher, was syndicated to 300 newspapers in the early 1900s. Pleasant Run Creek flows through Irvington, where other landmarks include Howe High School (which opened in 1938) and the Bona Thompson Memorial Center, the last surviving Butler building. Today, it is a cultural, arts, and civic center.

c. 1945

BRIGHTWOOD

Station Street today is a mere ghost of a once-thriving commercial block

LEFT: Station Street was the business hub of the Brightwood neighborhood in the Northeastside area during the 1940s when this photo was taken. Initially settled in the 1870s by railroad workers employed at repair shops in the area, Brightwood was soon incorporated as a town. The area consisted primarily of foreign-born and first-generation residents of Irish, German, and British ancestry. It shared a boundary, Martindale Avenue, with the neighborhood of Martindale to the west. Brightwood was annexed into Indianapolis in 1897; about ten years later, several railroads relocated their repair yards to Beech Grove. African Americans gradually became the primary residents of Brightwood. Schools also became a hub of activity for local residents. In 1935, the PTA at School 37 was the first at an African American school to become part of the National Congress of Parents and Teachers.

ABOVE: Although many businesses have pulled out of the Brightwood neighborhood since the 1960s, the neighborhood retains a sense of pride for several reasons. About one block south of the Station Street area in this photo is Martin University, a private, nonprofit college attended by about 500 students. Martin University was created to serve low-income, minority, and older students. In 1986, Martindale Avenue was renamed Dr. Andrew J. Brown Avenue. After marching with Martin Luther King Jr. in Selma, Alabama, Brown helped found the Indiana Black Expo, a summer celebration of African American heritage and achievement that is the largest event of its kind in the country. Today, even as Brightwood and Martindale continue to face economic challenges, the neighborhoods are the home of about eighty churches, including many storefront churches.

1907

GRIFFITH BLOCK/
CIRCLE CENTRE MALL
The ornate historic facade has been
retained for this modern mall

LEFT: In 1872, the Griffith Block Building was designed
in the Venetian Commercial Italianate style and erected
on West Washington Street. For decades, the limestone
building housed the offices of the *Indianapolis News*,
which can be seen on the street level in this photo
taken in 1907. The *News*, an afternoon newspaper, was
owned (secretly) during this period by former U.S. vice
president Charles Fairbanks. A wealthy Republican who
served under—and clashed with—President Theodore
Roosevelt, Fairbanks did not want Indianapolis
residents to regard him as an all-powerful force in
town. His ownership of the *News* wasn't revealed until
after his death in 1918. His three sons followed him as
publisher until the newspaper was purchased by the
Indianapolis Star's owner, Eugene C. Pulliam, in the
late 1940s.

c. 1977

RIGHT: With the construction of Circle Centre in the 1980s, the Griffith facade became one of eight historical facades incorporated into the mall. The historic limestone facade was moved across the street in 1995 so that it could be part of the mall, which, unlike many suburban malls built during the 1980s and 1990s, has a variety of different fronts instead of being a monolith. Along with facades of the other historic structures (including the Rost Jewelry store built in 1887 with later art deco modifications), the Griffith facade was incorporated into Circle Centre as a tribute to downtown's historic role as the state's retail center. The four-level mall occupies two entire city blocks.

LEFT: The building survived beneath twentieth century additions at odds to its Italianate design.

1949

UNION STATION
At the "Crossroads of America"

ABOVE: In its heyday, thousands of passengers bustled daily through Union Station, at 39 Jackson Place, from soldiers (and their teary sweethearts) during World Wars I and II to college students and vacationers. Legendary trains such as the *Spirit of St. Louis* that roared through Union Station helped spur the "Crossroads of America" nickname for Indianapolis; at the station's peak, more than 200 trains came through each day. The snow-white Santa Claus in the photo from 1949 was a fifty-one-foot-high "Santa Colossal" made of Styrofoam. He "spoke" recorded Christmas greetings to visitors at the Indianapolis Industrial Exposition; postcards with this image were handed to thousands of yuletide passengers at the terminal. When efforts to find a permanent home for Santa failed, he was chopped up to become insulation.

BELOW: The Romanesque Revival Union Station was completed in 1888. It replaced an earlier depot built in 1853 on the same site and known as the first Union Station in the world.

c. 1900

76

ABOVE: This former concourse, or "head house," was nearly demolished, along with the rest of the train terminal, in the early 1970s. With the decline in passenger rail service, traffic at Union Station had nearly vanished and Penn Central, the station's owner, filed for bankruptcy. A New Year's Eve party in late 1971 was staged to raise money to save the station, which eventually was placed on the National Register of Historic Places. The bumpy path continued, though, even after a $30 million restoration in which Union Station reopened in 1986 as a "festival marketplace" of boutiques and restaurants. The concept fizzled and the city government searched for new buyers. In 1999 Crowne Plaza leased the facility for a banquet hall and conference center.

1928

TRIPP WAREHOUSE / LUCAS OIL STADIUM

The replacement for the Hoosier Dome was built on the site of a bygone warehouse

ABOVE: The eight blocks that later became the site of Lucas Oil Stadium contained a mixture of businesses and houses, as was typical before city zoning laws regulated the use and location of buildings. Within the footprint of the stadium once stood seventy-two houses, mainly frame doubles with a sprinkling of stores. As the decades progressed, industrial buildings replaced many homes on Senate Avenue and Willard, Empire, and Henry Streets. The Tripp Warehouse Company, seen here in 1928, was

founded by Ernest H. Tripp and operated by his wife Anna after his death in 1920. It sat south of the stadium at 620 South Capitol Avenue among a cluster of businesses fed by railroad spurs. Meandering through the site was Pogue's Run, a creek named after settler George Pogue who disappeared in 1821 and presumably died at the hands of Indians. In 1915 the stream was routed underground from East New York Street to White River in an improvement project that cost over one million dollars.

ABOVE: Lucas Oil Stadium, home of the popular Indianapolis Colts, opened in 2008 following the team's victory one year earlier in the Super Bowl. With a retractable roof and a seating capacity of 63,000, the stadium replaced the RCA Dome (initially known as the Hoosier Dome), which was located about one block to the north and built just prior to the move of the Colts in 1984 to Indy. The namesake of Lucas Oil is multi-millionaire Forrest Lucas, a native Hoosier who grew up poverty-stricken but went on to create an enormously successful type of motor oil. The new stadium was a key factor in the NFL's decision to select Indianapolis to host the Super Bowl in 2012, a historic first for the city. Although the Colts did not play in that game (the New York Giants beat the New England Patriots), the hometown team continually expands its fanbase, with quarterbacks Peyton Manning, followed by Andrew Luck, enjoying almost iconic status.

CENTRAL CANAL

A major cleanup transformed this city eyesore into a sparkling attraction

c. 1953

LEFT: Looking east, the view in the 1950s of the Central Canal just beyond West Street took in the dome of the Indiana Statehouse, but little else of significance except for the grim smokestacks of paper mills that dominated the area. At this time, the Indiana State Museum was located in the basement of the Statehouse. Most of its displays were of artifacts related to natural history. After much public clamor to upgrade the state museum, in 1967 it moved into the neoclassical building on North Alabama Street, which once served as the Indianapolis City Hall. The view from this spot on the canal, though, would not have changed much in those thirty years. The Indianapolis Water Company owned the canal; the southern area around its banks just beyond the Mile Square was not considered ripe for development.

BELOW: The Indiana Statehouse is visible as ever from the vantage point of the Central Canal. To the right is part of a spectacular structure that's been generating plenty of buzz since its grand opening in 2002. It's the $105 million Indiana State Museum, which is split into two buildings on the east and west banks of the canal, bridged by a 200-foot walkway. Built of Hoosier limestone and sandstone, the museum serves as a kind of monument to the state, beginning with its main lobby that features a fifty-five-foot-tall sculpture spelling "INDIANA" by artist Robert Indiana. The museum's artifacts range from Amish quilts and T. C. Steele paintings to a re-creation of the beloved L. S. Ayres Tea Room. The area around the canal became a pedestrian park.

1928

WALKER THEATRE

The vision of an African American millionaire who would never see her creation

LEFT: A magnificent, four-story building on Indiana Avenue was the vision of one of the most remarkable women in Indiana history. Madam C. J. Walker, whose parents were slaves, may have been the first African American woman to become a millionaire, but she didn't live to see the completion of the building complex that she envisioned. She amassed a fortune as an entrepreneur in the hair-care and cosmetics industry, but died eight years before the Walker Building opened in 1927. The building, shown here in 1928, served as the international headquarters for the Walker family's business. It also housed popular restaurants (including one called the Walker Coffee Pot), a beauty college, a ballroom, and a drugstore. During the 1940s and 1950s, the Walker Building was the hub of vibrant Indiana Avenue, the center of African American music and business life in Indianapolis.

ABOVE: Just as in the heyday of the Indiana Avenue jazz scene, the building named in honor of Madam Walker is a symbol of ethnic pride today. The Madam Walker Urban Life Center includes the majestic Madam Walker Theatre Center, which seats about 950 people. The theater is decorated with elaborate carvings celebrating African folklore and culture. The center opened in 1988 after a massive restoration of the former Walker Building, which had deteriorated during the 1970s as businesses left Indiana Avenue. The trend has reversed, and the Walker Theatre is a popular setting for a range of civic events. They include festivals that pay tribute to the late jazz legend Wes Montgomery, the biggest star to emerge from the Indiana Avenue music scene.

c. 1935

WESTSIDE HOUSES / LOCKEFIELD GARDENS
Low-income housing replaced by modern apartments

ABOVE: Future basketball star Oscar Robertson described his boyhood neighborhood of the 1930s as a "ghetto" in his autobiography. Federal officials used the phrase "slum clearance" during the 1930s, when this photo was taken, to refer to the work undertaken in the Westside to make way for Lockefield Gardens. Almost 400 houses near Indiana Avenue and Locke, North, and Blake Streets, including the homes here, were removed to build Lockefield Gardens, the first major public housing project in the city. Generally regarded as one of the most successful of such developments in the nation, Lockefield Gardens opened in 1938 and consisted of 748 living units, primarily low density apartment groupings. The project was funded by the Public Works Administration as part of the New Deal during the Depression.

ABOVE: Lockefield Gardens is a mix of original buildings from the late 1930s that have been renovated and modern residences constructed in the 1980s and 1990s. Well landscaped and well maintained, the apartments in Lockefield Gardens have become popular among college students, particularly with the growth of nearby Indiana University–Purdue University Indianapolis (IUPUI). Many of Lockefield Gardens' older buildings, which were upgraded in a "soft rehab" technique, have their original casements. Before the revitalization of Lockefield, the housing units had fallen into disrepair as middle-income families moved farther north or west. Lockefield, though, never deteriorated to the "ghetto" of Robertson's youth.

1941

OUTHOUSE / IUPUI CAMPUS CENTER

The hub of IUPUI is located on the former site of an infamous two-story outhouse

ABOVE: When this photo was taken in 1941, a time when most Indianapolis residents had been enjoying indoor plumbing for decades, this two-story outhouse, located at 458–460 North Agnes Street, still stood tall, if not proud, behind an apartment building. This was in the Near Westside area, which comprised of several poverty-stricken neighborhoods. Much of the area that is now the site of Indiana University-Purdue University Indianapolis (IUPUI) was described as "a shameful mile of shambles" by the *Indianapolis Star* in the early 1950s. The blighted neighborhoods, which also included an outhouse near a shallow well that provided drinking water for residents, were about a mile from the Soldiers' and Sailors' Monument. However, the apartment buildings and outhouses were tucked away on little used dirt streets, so they were seldom seen by those who worked downtown.

ABOVE: Out with outhouses, in with IUPUI, one of the nation's largest urban campuses. The site of the former outhouse today is the IUPUI Campus Center, which opened in 2008 in the 400 block of University Boulevard. (The name was changed from Agnes Street in the 1980s.) The hub or "living room" of the campus, the spacious building includes public spaces, lounges, food services, a cultural arts gallery, a credit union, and a bookstore. Since IUPUI's beginnings in the late 1960s, it has grown dramatically, both in student population and buildings. Today, IUPUI is attended by more than 30,000 students, making it the third largest campus in the state behind only its "parents," Indiana University and Purdue University, which are long-time rivals. IUPUI also has become one of the largest employers in Indianapolis.

c. 1925

RIVERSIDE AMUSEMENT PARK

A beloved amusement park which captivated generations of Hoosier families

ABOVE: Generations of Hoosier children first experienced the thrill of riding a roller coaster, Ferris wheel, and a waterslide at Riverside Park, which flourished for more than sixty years along the White River at West Thirtieth Street. The amusement park opened in 1903 next to farmland that Mayor Thomas Taggart asked the city to purchase in the 1890s as part of a series of public parks. Riverside, shown here in the mid-1920s, initially offered only a handful of "fun house" rides, as well as a toboggan. Eventually, the amusement park captivated families with a miniature railroad and two roller coasters called the Flash and the Thriller. In 1952, Riverside was visited by more than a million patrons. It was not all fun and games though. Riverside generated outrage by clinging to a "whites-only" admission policy through the 1950s even as African American families moved into surrounding neighborhoods.

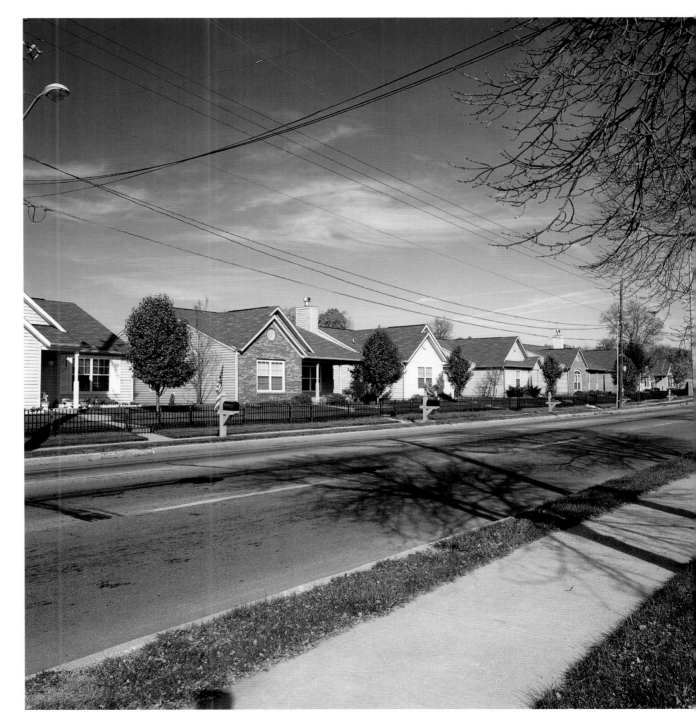

RIGHT: Several factors contributed to the demise of Riverside Amusement Park, which closed in 1970 after years of deterioration. Middle-class residents had abandoned Riverside and other neighborhoods in favor of new subdivisions farther north. In addition, the construction of Interstate 65 through the nearby area hurt property values, at least temporarily. Since 2000, several residential subdivisions, including River's Edge, have been built on or next to the site. Most of the new homes and town houses are on the north side of West Thirtieth Street near Riverside Parkway Drive. To the south, Riverside Park and Golf Course emerged in the 1980s after the city launched a rejuvenation effort. The Major Taylor Velodrome, a $2.5 million cycling track named for a famous African American cyclist from Indianapolis, is also located here. It seats 5,000 spectators.

c. 1915

INDIANAPOLIS MOTOR SPEEDWAY
The Indianapolis 500 flourished after bumpy beginnings

LEFT: The Indianapolis Motor Speedway Corporation was formed on February 9, 1909, when 328 acres of farmland northwest of downtown was purchased by flamboyant entrepreneur Carl Fisher and his partners. A two-and-a-half-mile oval track was built and the first car race, a five-mile dash, was held in August 1909. It was a disaster. The track surface broke up, causing the deaths of two drivers, two mechanics, and six spectators. After several unsuccessful automobile and motorcycle races, Fisher decided a single extravaganza was needed. The Indianapolis 500 was born with great success on May 30, 1911. Ray Harroun beat the other thirty-nine drivers, winning the race with an average speed of 74 mph in six hours and forty-two minutes.

ABOVE: The Indianapolis Motor Speedway has been nicknamed the "Brickyard" since 1909, when the surface of the two-and-a-half-mile oval track consisted of 3.2 million bricks. A single strip, called the "yard of bricks", remains at the track's start/finish line. The Indianapolis 500, which today has a field of 33 cars, became and remains the largest single-day sporting event in the world, regularly drawing about 250,000 spectators to the Speedway. A new digital scoring pylon was built in 2014 as part of extensive improvements, including enhanced video boards for spectators. Now the Speedway also hosts other races. Since 1994, NASCAR has held the Brickyard 400, featuring stock cars. And the Grand Prix of Indianapolis, a road race involving Indy cars, debuted in 2014.

1924

THE LINE UP

PRES-O-LITE BATTERIES

INDIANAPOLIS MOTOR SPEEDWAY

Over a century, Indianapolis has firmly established itself as the home of American motorsport

ABOVE: An eye-catching pagoda housing racetrack officials was a landmark at the Speedway for decades, but fate was not kind to it. The wooden, Japanese-style pagoda, seen here in 1924, was painted green and white; it burned to the ground in 1925 the day after the Indianapolis 500. The pagoda had become such a landmark that a second one, also wooden, was erected immediately. By the mid-1950s, the Speedway began to take on a modern look as aluminum and steel seats supplanted aging wooden

grandstands. The second pagoda was replaced by the modernistic Tower Terrace. Propelled to a new era of glory, the Speedway attracted the best drivers from around the world. Mario Andretti, Jim Clark, Graham Hill, Jacques Villeneuve, and Emerson Fittipaldi are among those who have won the world's premier car race and claimed the massive Borg-Warner Trophy that goes with the Indy 500 title.

ABOVE: A towering new pagoda was completed in 2000 as part of a series of changes at the Speedway. The Tower Terrace built in 1955 was demolished to make way for the new pagoda, which is 153 feet tall. Indianapolis architect Jonathan Hess created a pagoda as a tribute to the racetrack's heritage. In addition to the debut of NASCAR and the Grand Prix of Indianapolis, other changes have unfolded at the Speedway.

The infield had been the setting for rollicking party behavior from the 1950s through the 1980s, with the most notorious section known as the "snake pit." Beginning in the 1990s, the Speedway strived for a more wholesome image, with increased security, more bleachers in the infield, and upgraded concessions.

FEDERAL BUILDING

This massive neoclassical structure kicked off a trend in city architecture

1908

LEFT: The structure that spans a city block of Ohio Street between Pennsylvania and Meridian Streets became known as the Federal Building, although it was officially called the U.S. Courthouse and Post Office. The $12 million construction of the neoclassical structure began in 1903. Built of Indiana limestone, the Federal Building is lined on all sides by Doric columns. The grand architectural style, which combined Greek, Roman, and Renaissance classicism, started a trend in public architecture in Indianapolis. Massive structures influenced by the Federal Building include the Indianapolis Public Library built in 1917. The south facade of the Federal Building, seen here in 1908, features several large sculptures. The interior has mosaics, murals, and stained-glass windows in the courtrooms. Until 1973, the Federal Building housed the city's main post office.

BELOW: In 2003, the federal courthouse was renamed as part of its centennial anniversary celebration. The Birch Bayh Federal Building and U.S. Courthouse no longer houses the post office, but it remains the imposing home of the courtrooms for the U.S. District Court of Southern Indiana. A U.S. senator from 1963 to 1981, Birch Bayh was the author of some important constitutional amendments. The former Federal Building has often been confused with the Federal Office Building (also known as the Minton-Capehart Building) at 575 North Pennsylvania Street. Erected in 1975 in the modern architecture style, its structure is frequently derided for its wavy exterior bands of orange and other vivid colors.

INDIANA SCHOOL FOR THE BLIND / AMERICAN LEGION MALL

Opened in 1853 on the block bounded by North Meridian and Pennsylvania Streets

1925

FAR LEFT: By 1925, when this photo was taken, the Indiana School for the Blind had occupied prime real estate in the Mile Square for more than seventy years. Set far back from North Street and surrounded by iron fences, the school's five-story building with Corinthian cupolas opened in 1853 in the block bounded by North Meridian and Pennsylvania Streets. Over the years, a barn, dormitory, laundry, and greenhouse were added to the grounds. During the 1920s, though, Hoosier politicians decided the downtown site was ideal for a war memorial plaza, meaning the school would have to close at this location. The current Indiana School for the Blind building opened in 1930 on sixty acres at North College Avenue and Seventieth Street. The new school incorporated the iron fence and stone scrolls from the downtown structure.

BELOW: In the wake of World War I and with returning doughboys swelling its ranks, the American Legion was founded in 1919 and chose Indianapolis for its headquarters. The legion lobbied for creation of a five-block war memorial that would include its headquarters building as well as various tributes to fallen soldiers. It took most of the 1920s to construct the memorial plaza and structures, which were primarily built of Indiana limestone and marble. The American Legion National Headquarters, designed in a totalitarian classic style, opens onto a terraced mall show here. Rising up in the background is the Indianapolis Public Library's vast, five-story addition that opened in 2007.

c. 1943

LEFT: This horse-drawn Indianapolis Brewing Company wagon, advertising war bonds during World War II, poses on North Street in front of the American Legion.

c. 1860

MARION COUNTY SEMINARY / UNIVERSITY PARK

The former school of *Ben-Hur* author Lew Wallace

ABOVE: Marion County Seminary opened in the 1830s and chalked up a rather illustrious list of alumni. They included an indifferent student who was the son of David Wallace, Indiana's governor during the late 1830s. Lew Wallace later became the state's best-known Civil War leader, then reaped astonishing success as the author of *Ben-Hur* (1880), which historians believe was read by more people in its era than any book other than the Bible. As a student at Marion County Seminary, Lew Wallace indulged in a "habit of truancy," as he put it later. Known for its rigorous curriculum, Marion County Seminary was overseen by an elected board of trustees. Its building in University Square was demolished in 1860 as the public school system in Indianapolis began to flourish.

ABOVE: University Park was so named because civic leaders in 1821 expected a state university to develop on the site. It never happened and instead the park became the setting for several statues, as well as the five-level DePew Fountain at the park's center. Among the statues in University Park, which was created after a community-wide fund-raising effort, are sculptures of Presidents Abraham Lincoln and Benjamin Harrison, the wood nymph Syrinx, the satyr Pan, and Vice President Schuyler Colfax, who hailed from South Bend and served under President Ulysses S. Grant. Colfax socialized with the Lincolns and is believed to have been the last public official to shake the president's hand.

1932

INDIANA WAR MEMORIAL

Homes and churches were demolished to create the memorial and plaza

LEFT: The Indiana World War Memorial Building, seen here in 1932, sits on a block raised above street level, meaning the shrine itself rises 210 feet above the ground. Constructed during the 1920s, the war memorial and surrounding plaza were initially designed to honor the sacrifices of Hoosiers who had fought in World War I. To create the memorial, several structures were removed from the two city blocks bounded by Vermont, Meridian, Pennsylvania, and North Streets. The north and south sides of the shrine have majestic doors of double-leaf bronze. General John J. Pershing, a World War I commander, laid the cornerstone of the three-story memorial building on July 4, 1927, declaring it "a patriotic shrine." The memorial has a 500-seat auditorium, a grand staircase, and a Shrine Room that symbolizes peace and unity.

RIGHT: Today the Indiana War Memorial has come to symbolize the sacrifices of all Hoosiers who have fought in modern wars. Inside are listed the names of every Hoosier who participated in World War I, as well as all of those killed or missing in action in World War II, Korea, and Vietnam. Names are being added of Hoosiers killed in the 9/11 tragedy and the wars in Iraq and Afghanistan. Another majestic Indianapolis landmark is also clearly visible in the photo, the Scottish Rite Cathedral at 650 North Meridian Street. The world's largest Scottish Rite cathedral, the Tudor building with Gothic ornamentation was completed for $2.5 million in 1929. The cathedral is laid out in multiples of thirty-three feet to symbolize the thirty-three years of Jesus Christ's life. The cathedral's Gothic tower, which rises 212 feet above the street, has a carillon of fifty-four bells, making it one of the country's largest.

1862

SULLIVAN HOUSE / MERIDIAN STREET METHODIST CHURCH

The home of an early Indianapolis civic leader

ABOVE: As befitting a mover and shaker, early Indianapolis civic leader William Sullivan (1803–86) lived in a stately and spacious home, seen here in a photo from 1862. A civil engineer and educator, Sullivan became a county surveyor. He oversaw street improvements, designed city maps, and helped get the local school system up and running. If all that wasn't enough to keep him busy, Sullivan also served as the city council president, became a justice of the peace, and was on the board of trustees for railroads. He couldn't have slept much, but when he did it was at this house on the northwest corner of North Meridian and St. Clair Streets. Sullivan undertook all of these public and private endeavors after moving to the still-new city of Indianapolis in 1834. The limestone structure on the former site of William Sullivan's mansion was built as the Meridian Street Methodist Church in 1901.

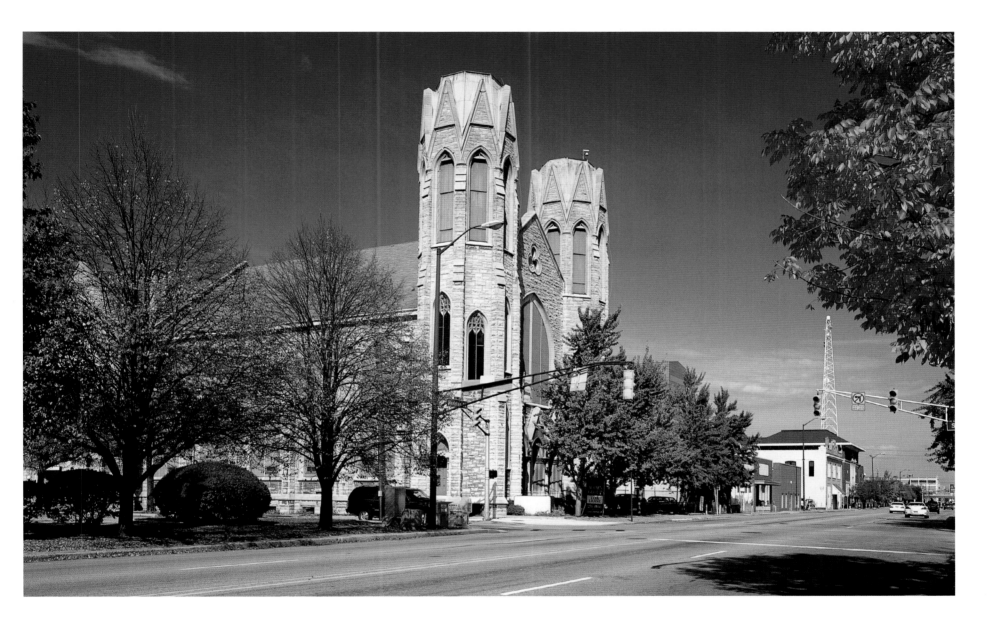

ABOVE: Since the late 1940s, when the church moved much farther north to the 5500 block of North Meridian, the building has had two very different uses. First, the structure became the flagship of the Indiana Business College. Because college officials regarded the building as a temporary home, they made only minor alterations to the interior, which included a sanctuary – even though the structure remained a business college for more than fifty years, longer than it was a church. With enrollment increases, the college, now known as Harrison College, moved in 2003 into a larger structure on East Washington Street. The former church-turned-business college structure was converted into condos. The condos have arched Gothic and cathedral windows, reminders of the house of worship heritage.

1925

CITY MARKET AND TOMLINSON HALL

Both the City Market Building and Tomlinson Hall dated back to 1886

c. 1910

LEFT AND ABOVE: The street scene from 1925 depicts a bustling market day at City Market, which was built in 1886 and adjoined Tomlinson Hall (both on left of the main photo). An enormously popular marketplace for fresh fruit, vegetables, meat, bread, and poultry, City Market had produce stands run by generations of immigrant families. Just west of the market, Tomlinson Hall, also built in 1886, was a massive civic building at the corner of Market and Delaware Streets. With a brick facade and detailing of limestone, Tomlinson Hall featured a stage and spacious performing hall. The auditorium hosted political conventions, balls, lectures, and patriotic band concerts. Tomlinson Hall's dedication ceremony was timed during the Grand Army of the Republic Music Festival to raise money for the Soldiers' and Sailors' Monument. Tomlinson Hall was destroyed by fire in 1958.

RIGHT: A doorway arch from Tomlinson Hall survived the fire and was uncovered in the courtyard of City Market in 1977 during one of several renovations of the historic marketplace. Built with twin towers flanking a central entrance, City Market is a popular lunchtime destination for downtown workers, who "people watch" in the courtyard during balmy weather. From May through mid-October, a farmers' market is held every Wednesday; the bricked Market Street is closed to traffic so vendors can sell fruit and a colorful array of other fare. The courtyard is a frequent setting for pep rallies for the Indianapolis Colts and Indiana Pacers, as well as noontime music concerts.

1905

WHOLESALE DISTRICT, DELAWARE STREET

For several years the home of Colonel Eli Lilly's chemical shop

LEFT: Keach Fruit and Vegetable Market enjoyed a plum location in the middle of the Wholesale District when this photo was taken in 1905. A family-owned wholesale business founded in 1859, Keach and its bounty were on South Delaware Street just south of Maryland and Virginia Streets. The Wholesale District sprang up around Union Station after the Civil War so retailers would have easy access to railroads for their wares. For several years, the Wholesale District was the home of Colonel Eli Lilly's chemical shop, which the war hero opened in 1876. The small chemical business made medicinal syrups, sugar-coated pills, and fruit flavors. Other businesses in the Wholesale District included a millinery house, a grocery, and an electrical equipment company.

ABOVE: Buildings today near the former Keach Fruit and Vegetable site house people, not produce. Architects and engineers work in the brick building at the center of the photo. Stretching above the former Keach site is an enclosed walkway to Bankers Life Fieldhouse from a parking garage. The skybridge was designed with "retro architecture," just like the stadium for the Indiana Pacers. To the south of this site is the Alexander Hotel, a boutique hotel that opened in 2013 and was named after the once-obscure planner, Alexander Ralston, who laid out the city in the 1820s. Elsewhere in today's Wholesale District are dozens of restaurants, nightspots, delis and coffee houses. Eli Lilly and Co., of course, became a $6 billion pharmaceutical giant that has drugs distributed around the world. Even today, its international headquarters are not far from the Wholesale District, where it has its roots.

PENNSYLVANIA FREIGHT HOUSE / BANKERS LIFE FIELDHOUSE

This former freight depot became home to the Pacers

1919

LEFT: When this photo was taken in 1919, there were no signs that this would become the site of one of the city's top tourist attractions. The 100 block of South Pennsylvania Street, being near Union Station, was the location of a freight house for the Pennsylvania Railroad. One of four major Northeastern-based rail systems serving Indianapolis, its lines here—which connected to cities such as Terre Haute, Cincinnati, Frankfort, and Vincennes—operated until the late 1960s. This freight house was demolished in 1980. Before the 1980s, the Indiana Pacers played in Market Square Arena. The team, then a new member of the NBA after several years with the now-defunct American Basketball Association, was in danger of being purchased and relocated to another city. An exhausting sixteen-hour "Save the Pacers" telethon in 1977 is credited with rescuing the franchise.

BELOW: Bankers Life Fieldhouse is now immediately associated with pro basketball. The $183 million arena for the Indiana Pacers and Indiana Fever, which opened in November 1999, has a retro high school stadium appearance. The world's largest crane was used to install tresses on the stadium at 125 South Pennsylvania Street; the crane was so huge it had to be disassembled before being brought to the fieldhouse, then reassembled inside. With a seating capacity of 18,345, the fieldhouse doesn't just host pro basketball games. It's been a venue for major events ranging from concerts by Paul McCartney, opera stars and country music performers to ice shows and pro wrestling tournaments. A victory by the Indiana Pacers over the Boston Celtics opened the arena, which initially was known as Conseco Fieldhouse. Bankers Life, which occupies 6.2 acres, replaced the rather soulless Market Square Arena as the Pacers' home.

c. 1888

BENJAMIN HARRISON PRESIDENTIAL SITE

Indiana's only president resided here before he took office

ABOVE: In 1888, Benjamin Harrison (right) campaigned for president from his three-story, Italianate home at 1230 North Delaware Street, which he and his first wife, Caroline, had built fourteen years previously. A brigadier general during the Civil War and a U.S. senator, Harrison, a Republican, became the only president elected from Indiana. (His grandfather, William Henry Harrison, had been territorial governor of Indiana in the early 1800s, decades before being elected president while living in Ohio.) After the devastating year of 1892 – during a two-week period, Caroline Harrison died of tuberculosis in the White House, and her husband lost his bid for reelection – Benjamin Harrison returned to his Indianapolis home and resumed his successful law practice. This photo of the house was taken in about 1888. The L-shaped front porch was not added until 1896, three years after Harrison returned from Washington, D.C.

ABOVE: Most of the furnishings at the Benjamin Harrison Presidential Site belonged to the Harrison family. After returning to his home, Harrison remarried and started a new family; his daughter was only four years old when the former president died in 1901. Today, in addition to exhibits of historic artifacts inside the restored, sixteen-room house, the site includes special exhibits in a carriage house as well as captivating gardens with "vintage" flowers, plants, and herbs that, researchers have concluded, would have been popular during the era when Benjamin and Caroline Harrison were in residence. The presidential site is one of the gems of the neighborhood, now known as the Old Northside. Following decades of deterioration and the demolition of some historic mansions because of interstate highway construction, the Old Northside has been revitalized.

1928

SHORTRIDGE HIGH SCHOOL

Evolved from the city's first public high schools

ABOVE: Has any high school meant more to a community than Shortridge High has to Indianapolis? The alma mater of novelist Kurt Vonnegut (class of 1940), former U.S. Senator Richard Lugar, and author Dan Wakefield (both class of 1950) evolved from the first public high school in Indianapolis. Named after administrator Abram Shortridge, the high school conducted classes in downtown buildings before moving to Thirty-fourth and Meridian Streets in 1928, the year this photo was taken. Emphasizing academic rigor, Shortridge enjoyed national renown as one of the country's best public high schools. Booth Tarkington played hooky from Shortridge so frequently in the 1880s that his frustrated parents withdrew him; they sent the future Pulitzer Prize–winning author to an East Coast boarding school.

ABOVE: After being closed as a high school for nearly twenty years, Shortridge reopened in 2009. In a series of moves that would have intrigued Vonnegut and other editors of the school's *Daily Echo*—the first daily high school newspaper in the country—Shortridge had been closed in 1981. Three years later, it became Shortridge Middle school, attended by sixth through eighth graders in the Indianapolis Public Schools system before reopening as a high school. Wakefield used Shortridge—during its glory years—as the model for the high school in his 1970 best seller, *Going All the Way*.

1902

CROWN HILL CEMETERY

More vice-presidents are buried here than in any other cemetery

LEFT: Crown Hill Cemetery has several claims to fame. It's the third-largest graveyard in the country, it's the burial site of more American vice presidents (three) than any other cemetery, and it's the final resting spot of poets, business tycoons, and the gangster John Dillinger. This is how Crown Hill's southern portion, the superintendent's property, looked in 1902. The cemetery is located on such a tranquil, hilly area that city residents of the late 1800s and early 1900s came here to picnic. In creating the graveyard during the 1860s, civic leaders chose the site three miles northwest of the Circle because of its stunning vistas with oak, maple, and other deciduous trees. A three-arched Gothic gateway (pictured below) was constructed at the entrance on Thirty-fourth Street and Boulevard Place.

c. 1903

RIGHT: There is still plenty of burial space at Crown Hill Cemetery, which occupies 550 lush acres. Unusual or distinctive grave sites continue to be added more than 115 years after the nation's first lady, Caroline Scott Harrison, was brought here in a funeral procession following her death in the White House. The long-time owner of the Indianapolis Colts, Robert Irsay, is memorialized with a grave site that is unmistakable: a big horseshoe, the symbol of his football team. Ten governors of Indiana and one governor of Kentucky are buried at Crown Hill, which in the United States is exceeded in size only by cemeteries in Los Angeles and Cincinnati. In this photo of Crown Hill's southern portion, American flags decorate many graves in honor of Veteran's Day.

c. 1957

TEE PEE / STATE FAIRGROUNDS PARKING

Originally known as the Wigwam, it was a Native American-themed restaurant

ABOVE: When the Tee Pee first opened in the 1930s, it was originally known as the Wigwam. Among all the local restaurants that thrived during the drive-in craze of the 1950s, the Tee Pee was one of the most popular. The Native American–themed eatery with the unforgettable design enjoyed a high-visibility site next to the Indiana State Fairgrounds, off busy Fall Creek Parkway and East Thirty-eighth Street. The Tee Pee's heyday came during the late 1940s and 1950s when teenagers and college students were drawn to the drive-in to socialize and to enjoy a burger and milk shake. The Tee Pee was such a hit as a Northside hangout that a Southside Tee Pee opened on Madison Avenue. During the 1960s, the Tee Pee evolved into a more family-oriented eatery, offering Chief Burgers and feathered headdresses for children.

ABOVE: Drive-in restaurants suffered due to the soaring popularity of fast food during the 1970s. Even the Tee Pee bit the dust and was torn down in 1988 despite loud protests and various "stays of execution." For several years, its site has been a barren asphalt lot, a silent testament to a vanished culture. Today, it's been fenced and is used as an overflow parking lot for the state fairgrounds. Many other popular drive-in restaurants of the 1950s also closed or changed their formats. These included the Ron-D-Vu near the Butler University campus, the Pole at West Sixteenth Street and Lafayette Road, and several Knobby's Restaurants.

1927

BOOTH TARKINGTON HOUSE

North Meridian mansions include this Pulitzer Prize-winning novelist's home

LEFT: During the 1920s, the stately mansions along North Meridian Street became the showplaces of Indianapolis, not only for their grandeur but because many were the homes of literary notables and other celebrities. None were more famous than author-playwright Booth Tarkington (1868–1946), who lived in this Tudor-style home from 1923 until his death. His mansion at 4270 North Meridian (seen here in 1927) was older than many of his neighbors' homes; it was built in 1911 for Maria Hare, a widow with six children. After Tarkington bought and remodeled it, the mansion became the talk of the town. He filled it with an art collection and hosted glittering dinner parties for visiting luminaries such as Helen Hayes and the four Marx brothers, who arrived in a convoy of chauffeured white Cadillacs.

ABOVE: Still privately occupied, the Meridian Street mansions remain historical and architectural gems enjoyed by passing commuters and visitors. Thousands of commuters pass by daily because, unlike mansions in many cities that are tucked away on obscure streets or hidden behind gates, the North Meridian homes are on one of Indianapolis's busiest thoroughfares. The North Meridian mansions are a mix of architectural styles from French Renaissance and Italian Renaissance Revival to Southern Colonial, Colonial Revival, and Renaissance Revival. Almost all of them have elegant landscaping and towering trees. The Indianapolis Museum of Art uses the name of Tarkington's series of *Penrod* stories for its chic annual arts festival.

c. 1910

FAIRVIEW PARK / BUTLER UNIVERSITY
The Citizens Street Railway Company was the unlikely developer of Fairview Park

LEFT: The Citizens Street Railway Company was the unlikely developer of the 246-acre Fairview Park in 1890. By the start of the new century, Fairview Park (as seen in this photo from about 1910) had become an amusement park with a boathouse, band shell, ponies, and, eventually, a merry-go-round, bowling alley, and refreshment stands. Band concerts were Sunday afternoon staples and plays were staged in the summer on the canal's west bank. Fairview Park also served a role in health care during the early 1900s. Sick women and children, along with nursing mothers, were frequently brought to the park for fresh air and to enjoy the serenity of the flowers, trees, and ponds. During this era, Butler University was located in the Eastside suburb of Irvington, but the campus was rapidly outgrowing that site, which was hemmed in by upper-middle-class homes.

ABOVE: The campus of Butler University, a private university attended by more than 4,000 students, has been on the former Fairview Park site since 1928. Campus landmarks include massive Hinkle Fieldhouse, the largest basketball arena in the country when it was built in 1928 and the site of the boys' state basketball tournament for generations; the fortress-like Irwin Library; Arthur Jordan Hall, and Clowes Hall. Opened in 1855 as North Western Christian University, the college was founded by Ovid Butler, a prominent Indianapolis attorney and abolitionist. Today Butler is known for its instruction in music, pharmacy, education and broadcasting. Since making thrilling appearances in the NCAA's Final Four in 2010 and 2011, Butler basketball—and the bulldog mascot Blue—have become popular far beyond Indiana.

1908

BROAD RIPPLE

A site for entertainment and diversion, then and now

ABOVE: When this photo was taken in 1908, Broad Ripple was a self-governing town of several hundred residents along the Central Canal. During the summers, harried residents of Indianapolis traveled north by streetcars, and later interurbans, to tranquil Broad Ripple for relaxation and entertainment. With a park, shops, cruise boats that offered onboard dancing, and spots for fishing, Broad Ripple had the relaxed pace of a resort. Established as a town in 1836, Broad Ripple was annexed into the city of Indianapolis in 1922, by which point a housing boom of bungalows

was underway. Watt's Drug Store, seen in this photo along with Lodge No. 548 of the International Order of Odd Fellows (which occupied the top floor), gave way in 1925 to the fondly recalled Lobraico's Drug Store.

RIGHT: The family of Ivy and Mike Lobraico, shown in this 1931 snapshot, ran their corner drug store until 1990 when Mike turned ninety-five. The store then housed Chelsea's card and gift shop.

1931

ABOVE: With boutiques, nightclubs, ethnic restaurants, bars, antique shops, gourmet pet food stores and pizza parlors, Broad Ripple is often described as "quaint" because of its many specialty shops and outdoor cafes, Broad Ripple became a trendy destination for nightlife seekers in the 1980s and has remained popular, with continually escalating selling prices of the bungalows. The Broad Ripple Village Association is one of the city's strongest advocacy groups of merchants and residents. Lobraico's closed in 1990. Today, the historic building has businesses that typify Broad Ripple: Runners Forum, a locally-owned fitness apparel retailer, is on the sidewalk level. The Red Room, a nightspot with a dance floor, lounge and modern art décor, is on the upper level.

THE VOGUE

From a 1938 movie house to a 1977 nightclub

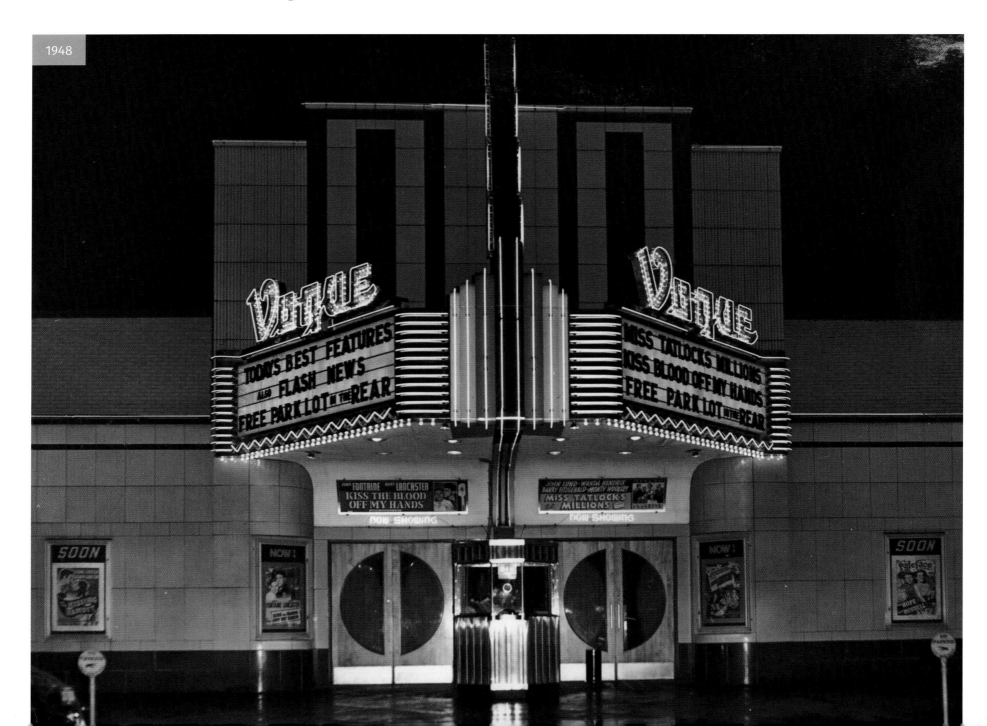

1948

LEFT: A landmark in Broad Ripple since it opened as a movie theater in 1938, the Vogue was developed by local cinema owner Carl Niesse. The name for the cream-colored, terra-cotta theater was suggested to Niesse by visiting movie stars Mary Pickford and Buddy Rogers. The first movie shown in the 800-seat theater at 6259 Broad Ripple Avenue was College Swing starring Bob Hope; admission was twenty-five cents for adults, fifteen cents for children. The Vogue was one of the first movie theaters in the Indianapolis area to be air conditioned. The marquee in this photo from the late 1940s resulted from a remodeling; at this point, the Vogue was considered one of the premier movie houses in the Midwest.

BELOW: Niesse sold the Vogue in 1954 and during the 1970s the theater showed adult movies. New owners pumped $500,000 into a restoration, paving the way for the Vogue's debut as a nightclub on New Year's Eve of 1977. As a nightclub, the Vogue is now one of the most popular venues in the Indianapolis area for dancing. Since a remodeling in 1993 that involved the installation of extensive lighting and sound systems, the Vogue has presented performances by the Red Hot Chili Peppers, the Dave Matthews Band, Little Feat, and Wynton Marsalis, as well as talent shows and regional band contests. With the remodeling in 1993, the size of the dance floor quadrupled. Long lines under the Vogue's marquee are a common sight as patrons wait to enter or buy concert tickets.

c. 1946

MONON RAILROAD / MONON TRAIL
The railroad line that morphed into a fitness trail

ABOVE: The Monon Railroad line began service to and from Indianapolis in the early 1880s, although its branch dated to 1865. The Indiana-based railroad ran between Louisville and Indianapolis as well as between Indianapolis and Chicago. When this photo of a train on the Monon tracks near Broad Ripple was taken, passenger service to Chicago included four round trips daily. Rumbling out of Union Station, the Monon line's service to Chicago was called the "Indianapolis Special," and sleeping cars were offered on an overnight train. Eventually, several railroad lines touted a service they called the "Indianapolis Special." With the decline in passenger rail service after World War II, the Monon shut down in 1959.

E HOOSIER" CROSSING THE NEW BRIDGE OVER THE WABASH RIVER, DELPHI, IND.

ABOVE: Today the Monon Trail is an enormously popular urban greenway for fitness and nature enthusiasts. The trail extends over fifteen miles from about Tenth Street near the Old Northside north to 146th Street in Carmel. Generally considered to be one of the busiest urban greenways in the country, the Monon Trail is often jammed with runners, cyclists, in-line skaters, and sightseers. According to some estimates, the Monon is used by more than 4,000 people daily. Grassroots citizens' campaigns helped initiate the development of the trail, which cost about $5.5 million to create. Funding came from several sources, including federal transportation grants and the Lilly Endowment. The Monon connects with other trails near the Central Canal, Fall Creek, and White River to form a major trail network through the Indianapolis metro area. The Monon Trail also connects to the city's Cultural Trail, an eight-mile trail linking cultural sites that was completed amid much fanfare in 2013.

c. 1918

FORT HARRISON / FORT HARRISON STATE PARK

One of the largest training sites for World War I troops

ABOVE: An active military facility for more than ninety years, Fort Benjamin Harrison was established in Lawrence Township in 1904, three years after the death of the president for whom it was named. The original site consisted of 1,994 acres. This photo from about 1918 or 1919 depicts soldiers who have returned from World War I, when the Indiana post became one of the country's biggest training and modernization sites. During World War II, thousands of Army troops were inducted at Fort Harrison, which trained finance specialists, cooks, chaplains, and medical technicians. Prisoners of war were housed at the fort's Camp Edwin Glenn. By the mid-1960s, Fort Harrison was the home of the Defense Information School and a huge Army finance center in a building that took up more than fourteen acres on East Fifty-Sixth Street.

ABOVE: Fort Harrison State Park is 1,700 acres of woods, trails, picnic areas, a sledding hill, ponds, shelter houses, and a golf course. Visitors enjoy observing everything from wildflowers to woodpeckers in their natural habitats. The park also has coffee shops and restaurants, including the Garrison, which is in the former dining hall for military officers. The vast park was created after Fort Harrison was phased out as a military facility over six years in the 1990s following the end of the Cold War. At the park's headquarters, visitors may tour the former prisons and military training camps. Some of the former military grounds were sold to private developers; they built suburban town houses and condominiums in 2000 and 2001.

c. 1974

KEYSTONE AT THE CROSSING / FASHION MALL

An upscale fashion hub

ABOVE: Far northern Marion County at Keystone Avenue and East Eighty-Sixth Street was farmland for all of the nineteenth century and more than half of the twentieth century. So when a shopping center complex initially opened in 1973, a distinctive, historic symbol, a farm silo, became its entry point. The retail center actually consisted of two adjacent shopping and restaurant areas linked by a glass archway, known as "The Crossing." One of the centers, called The Bazaar, was an unusually-designed labyrinth of boutiques and dining spots without walls. Patrons flowed among the open-concept retailers by use of ramps, balconies and stairs. The Bazaar concept did not endure, but the other portion of Keystone at the Crossing, the Fashion Mall, quickly flourished with its focus on luxury retailers. The anachronistic silo was demolished.

ABOVE: Saks Fifth Avenue, the New York City-based retailer of designer apparel, opened its first Indiana store at Keystone at the Crossing in 2003. By then, the Fashion Mall had long become a bustling destination for stylish shoppers from across a vast area, even including patrons lured from out of state. Other shops at the expanded Fashion Mall today include Tiffany & Co., Brooks Brothers, and Nordstrom. Instead of an interior décor with wood such as bamboo as in the bygone Bazaar, the renovated Fashion Mall is distinctive for its use of glass and a sleek appearance. Along with Keystone at the Crossing's popularity, East Eighty-Sixth Street has boomed; the retail corridor stretches to the east to the massive Castleton Square Mall, an area that, like Keystone at the Crossing, also had been semi-rural into the 1970s.

1928

FOUNTAIN SQUARE

The Fountain Square Theatre introduced Hoosiers to duckpin bowling

LEFT: Fountain Square was a bustling retail and entertainment district when this photo was taken in 1928. That year saw the opening of the Fountain Square Theatre in the district southeast of downtown at the intersections of Virginia Avenue, Prospect Street, and Shelby Street. Although the theater showed movies and presented vaudeville acts, it earned a permanent niche in Indianapolis history by introducing a sporting pastime to Hoosiers: duckpin bowling. Duckpin bowling—which involves small pins and balls—became a fad during the 1920s, with a bowling alley in the theater building. Fountain Square was known for the German heritage of its groceries, taverns, diners, and bakeries. The area eventually attracted Irish and Italian immigrants, with downtown customers visiting by streetcars. After World War II, though, Fountain Square declined as suburban shopping centers lured patrons away.

ABOVE: Antique shops, art galleries, and restaurants have opened in Fountain Square during a stunning revival that began in the 1990s. The Fountain Square Theatre Building, decorated with an Italian garden theme under a forty-foot dome ceiling with twinkling stars, was refurbished in 1998. Today the historic theater is used for a variety of events, including weddings, banquets, swing dancing, and receptions. Two duckpin bowling alleys are decorated with vintage bowling memorabilia and 1950s jukeboxes. The rejuvenated Fountain Square area includes an inn, a diner that serves milk shakes and tenderloins, and a Peruvian restaurant. The old streetcar tracks have been paved over.

c. 1882

BUDDENBAUM GROCERY / SANTORINI GREEK KITCHEN

Once a series of family retailers, now a popular restaurant

ABOVE: Fountain Square's two main commercial corridors–Virginia Avenue and Prospect Street–developed in the 1860s and this section of town became known as "the end" since it was at the end of the streetcar line. Located just a couple of blocks east at 1417 Shelby Street, this brick Italianate store dominated the corner and one can imagine neighbors gathering around a pot belly stove to gather goods and local gossip. Charles H. Buddenbaum (1860-1907) grew up in the grocery business

and in 1882 married the daughter of Frederick Ostermeyer of Severin, Ostermeyer and Company, one of the city's most prosperous wholesale grocers. At age twenty-two, Charles is first listed as proprietor of this grocery store, pictured in about 1882. Signage painted directly on the brick, as was popular during this era, identifies it as a Grocery & Tea Store.

ABOVE: Buddenbaum took a partner and moved his grocery to a nearby site in the 1890s. For many decades afterward the old grocery was occupied as a drugstore, including Clary's Laurel Pharmacy in the 1890s, Stuckmeyer Drugs in the 1910s and 1920s, John Cochran Drugs in the 1930s and 1940s, McKean Drugs in the 1950s, and Crescent Pharmacy in the 1960s. By 1975 the corner store housed Mills Furniture and Appliances. The Woodcutters' Bar occupied the one-story section in the 1980s. In 2001,

Taki and Jeanette Sawi, who first met on Santorini Island in Greece, opened Santorini Greek Kitchen in Fountain Square. They quickly needed more space so they moved to 1417 Prospect Street in 2004. The award-winning restaurant suffered a fire in 2010 but renovated the interior and is known today as one of the best Greek restaurants in town.

1935

GARFIELD PARK

The oldest park in the Indianapolis park system

ABOVE AND ABOVE RIGHT: Garfield Park on the Southside is the oldest park in the Indianapolis park system. The park traces its beginnings to 1873, when the city purchased the land from civic leaders who had created a harness racetrack known as Southern Park on ninety-eight acres. After President James A. Garfield was assassinated in 1881, the park was renamed in tribute. The pagoda was built in 1903 and served as the focal point for dances and other social gatherings. Southsiders also took pride in the original Garfield Park Conservatory, seen here in a photo from 1935. The greenhouse, which had been built twenty years earlier, lured visitors, as did the Sunken Gardens, which were dedicated in 1916, an amphitheater, and a swimming pool.

c. 1903

1915

ABOVE: A popular site for weddings, receptions, and dinner parties, Garfield Park Conservatory has been renovated substantially. Under a glass roof, the conservatory features plants native to the Caribbean and other tropical climates. It has a waterfall and a rain forest area that offer quite a contrast to the oaks, sycamores, and other trees native to Indiana that are found only yards away outside in the park. The Sunken Gardens also have been restored, with a goal of returning them to their glory days of the 1920s. The amphitheater and an arts center are settings for free performances by the Garfield Shakespeare Company. The main entrance to the park, which occupies about 122 acres, is at 2450 Shelby Street.

LEFT: Snapshot of the interior of the first Garfield Park Conservatory, taken shortly after its completion in 1915. The building was part of the park's master plan by landscape architect George Kessler. The original structure was replaced in 1954.

1911

BEECH GROVE

One of Marion County's self-governing communities

ABOVE: In addition to Speedway on the Westside, one of the self-governing communities within Marion County (incorporated Indianapolis) is Beech Grove on the Southeastside. The town had been incorporated for just five years when this photo, showing the Beech Grove Savings & Loan Building that dominated the 500 block of Main Street, was taken in 1911. Along with other businesses, the savings and loan opened because of the decision by the "Big Four" railroad to locate their automotive repair shops in the Beech Grove area, which had mostly been farms for cattle and various crops before 1905. Residents of Beech Grove elect a mayor and have their own school system and police and fire departments. After World War II, Beech Grove endured some economic setbacks as the train service declined nationally.

ABOVE: Nearly a hundred years after it was built—and long after trolley cars and horse-drawn buggies had vanished, except as novelties—the three-story office building on Beech Grove's Main Street remains largely unchanged. Today the former savings and loan building houses an investment firm, a barber shop, and other businesses. Recent revitalization includes a gateway to Main Street and removal of a three-foot concrete barrier wall on Emerson Avenue. The Main Street Reconstruction Project, completed in 2013, included improvements such as a bike lane, landscaping, and parking. According to the 2010 census, Beech Grove's population was 14,192.

SLIPPERY NOODLE

The state's oldest tavern and the city's oldest commercial building

BELOW: Founded in 1850, the Slippery Noodle Inn, seen here in a photo from the 1920s, is Indiana's oldest continuously operating bar on its original site. In its time, the inn has been through many name changes and scandals. Built as a roadhouse called the Tremont House, the tavern may have been a stop for escaped slaves on the Underground Railroad. In the 1860s its name was changed to the Concordia House, then to the German House. With widespread anti-German sentiment during World War I, the German House became Beck's Saloon. It was known as Moore's Beer Tavern during the Depression when John Dillinger, a local gangster, came to the bar with his cronies. Dillinger and his gang were indulging in target practice when they fired a shot, leaving a permanent bullet hole in the wall.

c. 1925

BELOW: Today the Slippery Noodle Inn is a 500-seat bar and restaurant, nationally known as a venue for blues music. "The Noodle" was rechristened in 1963 after the Yeagy family purchased the inn. They preserved its historic character but spruced up the place, both in appearance and reputation. About a decade before the Yeagys bought the tavern, a bordello had been operating upstairs. It closed after two patrons quarreled over a woman—one of the patrons pulled a knife and stabbed the other to death. With the Noodle's current renown for "hot blues" and its flamboyant past, it's a popular watering hole for visiting celebrities ranging from movie stars to race car drivers and NFL players. The Slippery Noodle is generally considered to be one of the oldest commercial buildings still standing in the Indianapolis metro area.

1925

INDIANA STATEHOUSE

The Capitol reflects its national counterpart in Washington, D.C.

ABOVE: Limestone from the Hoosier State, naturally, was chosen to build the Indiana Statehouse for $2 million in 1888. The cupola atop the glorious dome reaches 234 feet above the four-story Statehouse, also known as the Indiana State Capitol Building, seen here in a photo from 1925. With a design similar to the United States Capitol Building in Washington, D.C., the Statehouse dominates westward views from the Soldiers' and Sailors' Monument and Market Street. An eye-catching statue at the east entrance to the Statehouse depicts Oliver P. Morton, Indiana's charismatic governor during the Civil War. The interior of the Statehouse includes a central rotunda, regal columns, and marble galore. In addition to the governor's office and the chambers of the State Senate and State House of Representatives, the State Capitol Building houses the Indiana Supreme Court.

ABOVE: Imposing and impressive as ever, the Indiana Statehouse looks unchanged from 100 years ago. Actually, there have been several renovations of the Indiana State Capitol Building, including an $11 million project in 1988, but most of the upgrades and alterations have been to the interior. Rejuvenation of the surrounding downtown, however, have been very visible. The city once derided as "India-NO-Place" has exploded with growth and vitality. The population of Indianapolis (more than 848,780) makes it larger than Seattle, Baltimore, and even San Francisco. Its heartland location puts more than half the population of the United States within a one-day drive of the city.

INDEX